Working with Diversity in Youth and Community Work

:

- 5

D0549940

Titles in the Series

To order, please contact our distributor: BEBC Distribution, Albion Close, Parkstone, Poole, BH12 3LL. Telephone: 0845 230 9000, email: **learningmatters@bebc.co.uk**. You can also find more information on each of these titles and our other learning resources at **www.learningmatters.co.uk**

Working with Diversity in Youth and Community Work

SANGEETA SONI

Series editors: Janet Batsleer and Keith Popple

LearningMatters

First published in 2011 by Learning Matters Ltd

© 2011 Sangeeta Soni
British Library Cataloguing in Publication Data
A CIP record for this book is available from the British Library.

ISBN 978 1 84445 298 9

This book is also available in the following ebook formats:
Adobe Ebook: 9781844457816
EPUB: 9781844457809
Kindle: 9780857250315

Cover and text design by Code 5 Design Associates Ltd.
Project management by Newgen Publishing and Data Services
Typeset by Newgen Publishing and Data Services
Printed and bound in Great Britain by Short Run Press Ltd, Exeter, Devon

Learning Matters Ltd
20 Cathedral Yard
Exeter EX1 1HB
Tel: 01392 215560
info@learningmatters.co.uk
www.learningmatters.co.uk

I would like to dedicate this book to my father and mother – Rajinder Pal and Suraksh Kanta Soni.

Contents

Foreword from the Series Editors

Youth work and community work has a long, rich and diverse history that spans three centuries. The development of youth work extends from the late nineteenth and early twentieth century with the emergence of voluntary groups and the serried ranks of the UK's many uniformed youth organisations, through to modern youth club work, youth project work and informal education. Youth work remains in the early twenty-first century a mixture of voluntary effort and paid and state-sponsored activity.

Community work also had its beginnings in voluntary activity. Some of this activity was in the form of 'rescuing the poor', while community action developed as a response to oppressive circumstances and was based on the idea of self-help. In the second half of the twentieth century, the state financed a good deal of local authority- and government-sponsored community and regeneration work and now there are multi-various community action projects and campaigns.

Today, there are thousands of people involved in youth work and community work both in paid positions and in voluntary roles. However, the activity is undergoing significant change. National Occupation Standards and a new academic benchmarking statement have been introduced, and all youth and community workers undertaking qualifying courses and who successfully graduate do so with an honours degree.

Empowering Youth and Community Work Practice is a series of texts primarily aimed at students on youth and community work courses. However, more experienced practitioners from a wide range of fields will find these books useful because they offer effective ways of integrating theory, knowledge and practice. Written by experienced lecturers, practitioners and policy commentators, each title covers core aspects of what is needed to be an effective practitioner and will address key competences for professional JNC recognition as a youth and community worker. The books use case studies, activities and references to the latest government initiatives to help readers learn and develop their theoretical understanding and practice. This series then will provide invaluable support to anyone studying or practicing in the field of youth and community work as well as a number of other related fields.

Janet Batsleer
Manchester Metropolitan University

Keith Popple
London South Bank University

Introduction

I am fascinated by how people negotiate similarities and differences with others around them, in their personal and professional lives. As a Youth and Community Practitioner, early on, I realised the importance of conducting yourself with self-assurance, trust and genuineness, which I believe is crucial when negotiating differences between yourself and especially those who are different from you. In relation to the processes, particularly of developing relationships with others who are different from you, it is essential that you have a clear understanding of yourself – who you are, and most significantly, how you (in regard to your identity and culture) affect and impact on others, and understand how your perceptions, and the perceptions of others about you, potentially has a bearing on the nature of the relationships that you may develop. There is an old Buddhist saying, which I came across some years ago, that comes to mind at this point:

Someone who is confident in who they are, is more beautiful to the other.

It is therefore important to know who you are in relation to your individual identity, the result of all the myriad aspects of culture (including religious beliefs and practices, or not, as the case may be), that have helped to shape you. However, just as important, is the ability to appreciate and be open to difference. A Gandhian quote is helpful in this regard:

I do not want my house to be walled in on all sides and my widows to be stuffed. I want the cultures of all the lands to be blown as freely as possible. But I refuse to be blown off my feet by any. (Gandhi, 1921)

However, knowing yourself, let alone knowing others, is not easy. It is a study of a lifetime, and I find the metaphor of a 'journey of discovery' useful in this regard. This book is intended to support you part of the way through this journey, and I sincerely hope it will do so. I believe the ability to question is perhaps one of the most useful tools that you can take with you on this journey.

Along the journey, you will have many contradictory thoughts and feelings, and perhaps these will be accentuated by the interplay between the personal and the professional self.

There is an intentional focus on the self in the approach I have taken in this book, yet in our professional lives, we are constantly encouraged to act 'professionally', that means to make a serious attempt at being objective. I actually believe that the personal and professional inevitably inter-sect in our professional lives – it is unavoidable. In fact, perhaps it is only possible to be truly professional once you can understand how your 'self' influences the circumstances that you find yourself in. As Davies (2006, page 70) succinctly stated:

> *This confrontation with the personal within the professional is for me essential anyway. I start from the proposition that the two can never be wholly separated – that seeking to remove ourselves, our values, our perceptions and interpretations from our work, is never a realistic option.*

> *Ultimately 'practice' – youth work practice, more or less than any other – is delivered by and through the subjectivity of the human being. That subjectivity certainly needs to be checked and balanced by disciplined reflection and self-reflection. However it can never be eliminated, nor indeed should it be, since it is the carrier of the passion, the compassion and the empathy on which all good practice rides.*

However, in your questioning and self reflection, do not lose sight of the fact that there are different perspectives on most things – and as far as possible, especially as practitioners, we need to be open to the potential that another perspective is just as valid as our own – and perhaps sometimes even more valid than our own. This is a humbling thought, and I was helped to appreciate it by a Buddhist monk, who lived and worked in a Buddhist guest house in Delhi where I was staying for a few days, and where some of this book was written. The story which follows captures the complexity and importance of perception, how perceptions may be formed, and the judgements and actions it can lead to. In some ways, the story captures the essence, I hope, of what this book is intended to be about.

Here is the story as it was told to me by him:

> *There were two travellers, one following the other after a gap of a few hours. Both were travelling on the same road. As the first traveller was on the journey, it started to rain heavily. The traveller noticed a beautifully sculpted statue of the village deity, made from mud nearby, and thought, 'Oh dear, such beautiful work will be washed away by the rain.' So the traveller looked around, and all he could see was a large pair of slippers. He took the slippers and placed them carefully on top of the mud statue to protect it from the rain. Then the first traveller continued on the journey.*

> *Soon after this, the rain stopped, and the sun shone, and as this happened, the second traveller arrived at the place near the beautiful mud statue. This traveller was very shocked, and thought to himself, 'How can anyone be so ignorant and disrespectful as to place a pair of slippers on top of such a beautifully sculpted deity?' And so the second traveller quickly removed the slippers, before continuing on the journey.*

The Buddhist monk said, 'Both of them gained good karma for what each of them did, because they both acted from a good position'.

Returning to the task at hand, this book is the result of many years of personal and professional reflections on youth and community work practice in diverse communities. It is also based on many years of experience of training Youth and Community Workers. As such, the book consists of six chapters and a concluding chapter.

The first chapter in the book sets the scene and explores definitions of identity and culture and the links between these two concepts. As in all the chapters it includes practical exercises designed to enable practitioners/students to think about what is important for them with regard to their identity and culture, and how they would describe themselves as 'cultural' beings to those outside of their cultural group. It will help practitioners/students to understand the subtleties and complexity of cross-cultural communication, and their relationship to others that are similar or different from them.

The second chapter aims to examine and 'de-mystify' some of the language and terminology associated with working with diversity. For example, it considers what we mean by 'cross-cultural', 'inter-cultural', 'intra-cultural'; what is the nation state, class, ethnicity and race; and what is the relationship between these concepts? As in all the chapters, the practical exercises are designed to encourage practitioners/students to reflect and think about examples from their personal and professional experiences to illustrate the concepts.

In the third chapter, some theories and concepts that I think are particularly relevant to understanding working with diversity are explored. It includes developing an understanding of the impact and inter-play of power and authority in relation to the different cultural communities in any multi-cultural society.

The fourth chapter focuses on the notion of 'trust' as a foundational aspect of 'storying' – that is, the ability to tell your own story and to be able to listen to others'. It explores the idea that trust and the use of stories is an important aspect, not just of general professional practice, but especially relevant in the context of working with diversity.

The case of 'Islamophobia' as an example of prejudice, stereo-typing, social exclusion and marginalisation of particular groups in society is explored in the fifth chapter, bringing into focus and applying some of the concepts and theories discussed up to this point to a particular example from British society. The challenges posed by the rise in Islamophobia for practitioners are also identified.

In the sixth chapter, the last of the main chapters, some of the global forces (such as globalisation) that impact on the lives of young people and that clearly influence issues of power, authority and wealth distribution in the local and global contexts of their lives are explored, especially in regard to their relationship with race and class, and therefore in the context of working with diversity.

The Professional and National Occupational Standards for Youth Work (2010), and the Subject Benchmark Statement, Youth and Community Work (2009)

The relevant Professional and National Occupational Standards for Youth Work for each of the six chapters of this book will be listed at the beginning of the chapters.

However, in regard to the Subject Benchmark Statement for Youth and Community Work (QAA, 2009), I have listed the sections/points contained within the Statement, which are particularly relevant to the content of this book, in the discussion that follows. Please note that these are taken directly from the Benchmark Statement.

In relation to the values agreed in the Subject Benchmark Statement along with the National Occupational Statements (2009, 1.6, page 6), the following are of particular relevance to this work:

- It treats young people with respect, valuing each individual and their differences, and promoting the acceptance and understanding of others, while challenging oppressive behaviour and ideas.
- It respects and values individual differences by supporting and strengthening young people's belief in themselves, and their capacity to grow and change through a supportive group environment.
- It is underpinned by the principles of equity, diversity and independence.
- It recognises, respects, and is actively responsive to the wider network of peers, communities, families and cultures, which are important to young people, and through these networks, seeks to help young people achieve stronger relationships and collective identities, through the promotion of inclusivity.

It is generally accepted that there is a close and important relationship between Youth and Community Work.

The National Occupational Standards define community development work as follows:

The key purpose of community development work is to collectively bring about social change and justice, by working with communities to:

- Identify their needs, opportunities, rights and responsibilities
- Plan, organise and take action
- Evaluate the effectiveness and impact of the action
- And to do all these in ways which challenge oppression and tackle inequalities

(QAA, 2009, page 75, point 1.9)

The above statement of purpose, I believe, is very relevant to the content of this book.

Among the six values that underpin the community development work standards, three are of particular relevance to this book:

- Social justice: working towards a fairer society, which respects civil and human rights, and challenges oppression.
- Sustainable communities: empowering communities to develop their independence and autonomy, while making and maintaining links to the wider society.
- Reflective practice: effective community development is informed and enhances reflection on action (QAA, 2009, page 8, point 1.10).

Under the section on 'Defining Principles', the Benchmark Statement for Youth and Community Work (QAA, 2009, page 11) also refers to the NYA's statement of values and principles for Ethical Conduct in Youth Work (NYA, 2004), which lists four points. Two of the four points listed are of particular relevance to this work, and include to:

- Engage with (young) people with respect, and avoid negative discrimination.
- Contribute to the promotion of social justice among young people and in society generally, honouring diversity, yet identifying and challenging discrimination.

Under point 2.12 of the Benchmark Statement for Youth and Community Work (QAA, 2009, page 12), eight educational principles underpinning practice are stated; two of these are of particular significance here:

- Reflective: professionals and those involved as 'learners' or 'activists', are engaged in systematic reflection on their learning.
- Emancipatory: the education process is committed to personal, social and political empowerment/change.

As the Benchmark Statement (QAA, 2009, page 12, point 2.14) suggests:

- The purpose of youth and community work is to promote the education, development and flourishing of the young people, and communities with whom they work, in the context of promoting social justice.

It goes on to suggest that students of Youth and Community Work should be equipped to develop a strong sense of their professional identity, enabling them to engage with a variety of policy contexts, and with complex fields of accountability. It states four guiding principles to aid this process in students, one of which is to:

- Recognise the boundaries between personal and professional life.

This is also very significant in this work.

In the section on 'Working in and with Communities' (page 15), the subject Benchmark Statement (QAA, 2009), suggests, among other things, that students should explore:

- Power, empowerment and democratic learning and;

- Collective action and social changes, including enterprise and self-help strategies for addressing shared needs/aspirations, campaigning and links to social movements.

The exploration of the above for students/practitioners is relevant to the content of this book.

In relation to the 'subject-specific and generic skills' for Youth and Community Work, listed in the Benchmark Statements (QAA, 2009, pages 19–20), the following 'subject-specific skills' are relevant to all six of the chapters of this book:

5.1.1   Understanding, developing and managing their professional role.

- An understanding of, and the capacity to apply and integrate theoretical frameworks and key concepts, relevant to practice in youth and community work.
- Systematic analysis of relevant concepts, theories and issues of policy, and their use in informing practice.
- The ability to operate as a reflective practitioner, demonstrating appropriate professional actions and behaviour.
- Critical reflection upon, and commitment to, their continuing personal and professional development.

5.1.2   Fostering democratic and inclusive practice:

- The ability to create inclusive environments, and to identify and counter, oppressive attitudes, behaviours and situations, at both interpersonal and systemic levels.
- The capacity to build practice and an understanding of issues of power, empowerment, and the complexity of voluntary relationships.

5.1.4   Facilitating personal and collective learning development and capacity building:

- Skill in evaluation of the impact and effectiveness of their work and the work of community-based projects.

In relation to the 'Benchmark Standards' listed (QAA, 2009 page 24), the following are especially relevant to the contents of this book:

7.2   Graduates who have received a professional qualification should, in addition, typically be able to:

- Create and apply theories about practice and demonstrate practice skills as outlined in this statement.
- Practice ethically, recognising the complex, contested and essential nature of ethical practice in this discipline.
- Identify discrimination, oppression and/or exclusion, and be strategic in developing interventions to tackle these in different situations.

- Recognise and analyse powerful social policy and media discourses shaping practice, in order to work in the interests of young people and community group members.
- Operate as critical and reflective practitioners.
- Exhibit insight and confidence in managing themselves, and draw on conscious use of self, in working with others, and in leading or participating in teams.

Chapter 1
Identity and culture

Achieving your Youth and Community Work degree
The Professional and National Occupational Standards for Youth Work covered by this chapter are:

1.1.1   Enable young people to use their learning to enhance their future development

1.3.1   Facilitate young people's exploration of their values and beliefs

1.3.3   Enable young people to represent themselves and their peer group

2.3.2   Develop a culture and systems that promote equality and value diversity

5.1.1   Work as an effective and reflective practitioner

Introduction

This chapter explores definitions of 'identity' and 'culture' and enables students to think about what is important to them with regard to their own identity and culture.

The aim is for you to be more self-aware of the many influences in your life so that you can be more self-aware of the impact that you have when you intervene in the lives of others as youth and community workers. Essentially by understanding yourself more fully, and by understanding how others may perceive you, you become more skilled in understanding what is important in the lives of others with whom you work. This is at the heart of good youth and community work. The ultimate aim is, therefore, to better understand yourself and others (especially those different from you). However, this seems to be something that we struggle with.

As Rogers and Stevens (1967, page 93) point out:

> It is not surprising that we shy away from true understanding. If I am
> truly open to the way life is experienced by another person – if I can

take his world into mine – then I run the risk of seeing life his way, of being changed myself. So we tend to view this other person's world only in our terms, not in his. We analyse it and evaluate it. We do not understand it.

Good youth and community work demands that we both understand ourselves and how we impact on others, including those we are engaged to work with. Since no one person is the same as another and since the tapestry of life in fact ensures that diversity abounds in all its glory around us, it is inevitable that our encounters with others, personally and professionally, are fundamentally encounters with difference, with diversity. This chapter begins the journey of understanding these encounters.

The importance of identity

Identity is very important because at its simplest, it is about how a person understands themselves and how they make sense of their relationships with other people and with society in general. Therefore, the concept of identity encapsulates a sense of one's individuality while at the same time recognising the need for the individual's connections with others around himself/herself. As Woodward (1997, page 1) suggests, 'Identity gives us a location in the world and presents the link between us and the society in which we live'. Woodward (1997, page 1) also says:

> *Identity gives us an idea of who we are and how we relate to others and to the world in which we live'.*

The first of the following two activities will help you think about your relationship with others and help make some sense of how you feel about yourself and about these relationships. The second will help you think about and record key events/activities or people that have influenced and helped shape your identity.

ACTIVITY **1.1**

First, complete the sentences listed under the exercise titled 'Me'. Try and do this as instinctively as possible by writing the most important or first thoughts that come to mind when completing the sentences.

After you have completed the exercise 'Me', go on to think about and complete the table titled 'Identity Influences Timeline'.

'Me'

As a child I...
As a son/daughter I...
As a friend I...
As a youth I...
As a man/woman I would...
As a man/woman I could...
As a man/woman I need...
As a man/woman I should...
As a man/woman I might...
As a son/daughter I...
On the inside I feel...
On the outside I feel...
When I look at my life I...
Who I was is...
Who I am is...
Who I want to be is...
What I want in life is...
What I need right now is...
As a person I...

Identity Influences Timeline

Events and people who have influenced/impacted me

KEY EVENTS/ACTIVITIES	KEY PEOPLE	NOTES/COMMENTS
In childhood (to the age of 12)		
In my teenage years/my youth (to the age of 18)		
From 18 to 25		
From 25 to 35		
From 35 to 50		
After the age of 50		

It is important that you complete this exercise on your own, but then you may want to share it with one other person or with a small group.

These exercises can help an individual appreciate the importance of particular relationships and also help map the key events and people that have helped shape an individual's present identity. The second exercise particularly helps illustrate how both people and events can help shape who we are and what we value. An example of an event from my own life would include the fact that when I was a child my family migrated from Kenya to Britain, while a key relationship that stands out in my memory would be one with a close friend who was white and South African. I realise that both these have been particularly significant in shaping my values and therefore attitudes with regard not only to how I see myself (as an immigrant and member of Britain's ethnic minority population) but also to key issues in society such as immigration and the politics of race.

The notion of identity is inextricably linked with our self-image – how we see ourselves – and with our self-esteem – the extent to which we value ourselves. However, both our self-image and our notion of self-worth are often influenced by the 'messages' we receive from others. Those that we consider as significant in our lives can have a particularly strong influence on our levels of self-esteem/self-worth. How they perceive us seems to matter to us. These could include teachers, siblings, parents, relatives, colleagues, partners and children, among many others.

In short, our notions of self-worth can be directly affected by how others we have some contact with perceive us. This idea has its roots in the early work of Cooley (1998), who coined the concept of the *looking glass self* (pages 2 and 7). He suggested early on (in his work from 1902) that each individual continuously monitors how his/her self is reflected in the reactions of others. For example, if someone is rude to us, we may get upset or angry and react accordingly. If we are praised by others, then that may make us feel proud and increase our sense of self-worth/self-esteem. Thus, Cooley demonstrates how our self-image and sense of self-worth reflect how others react to us.

An individual's identity helps us understand and accept the ways in which we may be similar to others, but also marks our differences from others. As Woodward (1997, page 1) suggests, 'Identity marks the ways in which we are the same as others who share that position and the ways in which we are different from those who do not'. Head (1997, page 8), in fact, emphasises that, 'someone's identity distinguishes them from other people, it is a point of difference'.

This idea of having a sense of belonging to a group or community, or being conscious of one's differences from others, is important in how an individual's identity can be affirmed both by a sense of being similar to others and by being conscious of one's differences from others. Often, individuals from ethnic minority groups in Britain will speak about going 'back home' to where they clearly feel that their sense of belonging to and being part of the wider community, and therefore not being in a minority, is fulfilled. Class, culture and religious affiliation among other things may contribute to developing a sense of belonging and connection to others.

Although it is generally accepted, therefore, that our sense of self-worth and self-esteem can be affected by those that we have direct tangible links with, there are also other forces in society that can have an influence on our levels of self-esteem. For example, if the group or community we belong to is stereotyped negatively, for example by the media, then that too can reflect the self-worth of members belonging to that group or community (e.g. refugees, asylum seekers, homeless people, single parents).

Stereotyping is an example of a negative message that can have an adverse effect on an individual or a group's self-image and therefore self-esteem. Other examples of negative messages that can have an influence may include physical and verbal abuse, rejection, contempt, showing displeasure and lack of acceptance. This connection between an individual, his/her identity and a wider group/community or the wider society at large is at the heart of inter-cultural dynamics, that in turn are an inevitable aspect of our lives as the citizens of multicultural, multiracial Britain. Thus, understanding the importance of identity also leads to the need to understand how cultures can influence an individual's identity and how this in turn links the individual to a group or community with a whole sense of being, with a past and a future. This movement from the individual to the wider group or community shows how complex the connections between individual personal identity and groups in society can be.

> *A mature sense of identity means a sense of being at one with oneself as one grows and develops; and it means, at the same time, a sense or affinity with a community's sense of being at one with its future as well as its history or mythology.*

> (Erikson, 1974, pages 27 and 28)

This sense of belonging that an individual needs to feel with a wider group or community is particularly important as the individual (like all of us) lives in a fast and ever-changing globalised world. As Woodward (1997, page 51) points out:

> *Our cultural identities reflect the common historical experiences and shared cultural codes which provide us as one people, with stable, unchanging and continuous frames of reference and meaning beneath the shifting divisions and vicissitudes of our actual history.*

Yet, as individuals they are often also very conscious that they are, nevertheless, different from the very people with whom they have a sense of affinity and belonging and that they are perceived as such by the very people that they are or have gone to be among. In short, as an Indian woman, I never feel more British than when I am in India and yet I love being among the Indians in India.

Hall (1992, page 275) defines identity in a slightly different way. He suggests that the concept of identity has three different elements: '... those of the (a) Enlightenment subject, (b) sociological subject, and (c) post modern subject'.

The Enlightenment period in Western civilisation emphasised the possibility of human progress and the rational understanding of the social and natural worlds. As such, the individual was seen as a unified being who was capable of reasoning. A person's identity or sense of self consisted of having an inner core or self which remained constant and unchanging throughout life, and which meant that the person was considered to be in full control of his or her own actions and consciousness. Hall (1992) adopted this idea as one of the elements constituting his understanding of identity.

The second element, the idea of the 'sociological subject', builds on the idea that an individual forms a sense of himself/herself only through his/her interactions/ encounters with others. Thus, here the social elements of an individual's life are emphasised. As Hall (1992, page 276) points out:

> *Identity thus stitches ... the subject into the structure. It stabilizes both subjects and the cultural worlds they inhabit, making both reciprocally more unified and predictable.*

With the third element, the idea of the 'post modern subject,' Hall states that an individual is seen '... as having no fixed, essential or permanent identity ... The subject assumes different identities at different times, identities which are not uni-fied around a coherent "self"'.

This seems particularly relevant today in a world which is open to the forces of globalisation and therefore to the possibilities of rapid change. As a result, people may feel less grounded and may feel a sense of dislocation and fragmentation in their identities. Rapid social change can make people feel disrupted, leading to what Hall (1992) describes as a 'decentring' of subjects. As such, people may find it difficult to have a consistent sense of self and in fact are likely to feel that they have more than one identity – many identities, in fact. This can be potentially both a growth in a sense of disorientation and can be liberating (because it is now pos-sible to experiment with many identities).

ACTIVITY **1.2**

Read the story of a young schoolgirl and think about how the little girl shifts her identity depending on who she is with.

The story of a young schoolgirl

Once there was a young schoolgirl born in the city of Bradford in the north of England. Her parents had migrated from the district of Kashmir in Pakistan. One day she was asked to define her identity, by a researcher, and she answered:

When I am standing in the school playground with my English friends, I am Black. When an African Caribbean girl joins our group, I become Asian. When another Asian girl comes in, I think of myself as a Pakistani and a Muslim. When a Pakistani friend joins us, I become a Kashmiri, and when another Kashmiri girl turns up, I become a Bradford schoolgirl again.

So to sum up, the identity of individuals includes their sense of individuality and of being distinct from other people, and includes a need to feel special, a need to feel that they have roots and a need to actually feel comfortable with who they think they are.

Towards an understanding of culture

The word 'culture' is brandied around frequently, often in association with products and activities, and to describe environments in our society. Examples include the idea of cultural industries, cultural festivals and traditions, and organisations' cultures, but what does the concept of culture *really* mean; how important is it in our lives and therefore also in the lives of those with whom we work as youth and community workers?

ACTIVITY **1.3**

Think what the concept of culture means to you, and more importantly, think about what is important to you in your culture.

So, now think about how you would describe your culture; if someone simply asked you, 'What is your culture?', would you be able to answer this question easily, or would you struggle to answer it?

Why?

The concept of culture has many meanings, and it can be interpreted in numerous ways. In fact, Kroeber and Kluckhohn (1952) cited 164 statements that offered to explain what culture is, and Smith (1965) in his work in the West Indies suggested that there is 'no single correct definition of culture, although there is an impressive correspondence among many academic definitions'.

However, in the nineteenth century, Edward Tyler (1871), a British anthropologist, offered a widely accepted definition of culture as 'socially patterned human thought and behaviour'.

In fact, Kroeber and Kluckhohn (1952) devised a useful table listing the diverse definitions of culture (Table 1.1) (although this has been simplified and adapted).

In the end, Kroeber and Kluckhohn (1952, page 157) conclude that:

> *Culture is a product: is historical; includes ideas, patterns and values, is selective; is learned; is based upon symbols; and is an abstraction from behaviour and the products of behaviour.*

Given that the meaning of culture seems to be almost all-encompassing, it is not surprising that some anthropologists and sociologists seem to consider it synonymous to the idea of 'society'. In fact, Bodley (1997, page 10) says:

> *I use the term culture to refer collectively to a society and its way of life or in reference to human culture as a whole.*

Table 1.1 Diverse definition of culture.

Topical	Culture consists of everything on a list of topics, or categories, such as social organisation, religion or economy
Historical	Culture is social heritage, or tradition, that is passed on to future generations
Behavioural	Culture is shared, learned human behaviour, a way of life
Normative	Culture is ideals, values or rules for living
Functional	Culture is the way humans solve problems of adapting to the environment
Mental	Culture is a complex of ideas, or learned habits, that inhibit impulses and distinguish people from animals
Structural	Culture consists of patterned and inter-related ideas, symbols or behaviours
Symbolic	Culture is based on arbitrarily assigned meanings that are shared by a society

Adapted from Kroeber and Kluckhohn (1952)

It is, therefore, not surprising that Bodley (1997, page 10) suggests that:

> *Culture involves at least three components: what people think, what they do, and the material products they produce. Thus, mental processes, beliefs, knowledge, and values are parts of culture.*

Nadel (1951, pages 79–80) also seems to define culture as society:

> *Society means the totality of social facts projected into the dimensions of relationships and groupings; culture, the same totality in the dimension of action.*

It is no wonder, therefore, that the term is used widely in many contexts and can therefore be confusing. What adds to its confusing nature are the properties inherent in the concept. Bodley (1997, page 10) suggests

> *Culture also has several properties: it is shared, learned, symbolic, transmitted cross-generationally, adaptive and integrated.*

Therefore, because culture is transmitted and learned (from one person to another, and one generation to another), and not biologically inherited, it has within it the mechanism to change and evolve. I get very irritated when students come to a session on 'Working with Diversity' expecting to be told about the way to behave with and to understand a particular religion or cultural community in/with which they work. I have no doubt that I could quite easily describe the main features, for example, of Hindu culture (to which I belong), but the danger in doing so is that I will create the impression that all Hindus believe particular things and behave in particular ways. The danger is that I will stereotype them and forget that culture is ever-changing and fluid. Therefore, the communities and so the cultures that the people we work with, as youth and community workers, also change and evolve. In short, the Asian community in Britain today is not the same as the community that first arrived in Britain in large numbers in the 1950s and 1960s. It is this dynamic aspect of culture that leads to both bewilderment and wonder at its adaptive and fluid nature. However we choose to define it and understand it, culture is very important in our lives, because it is implicit in how we think and how we behave.

We are all products of cultural activity and evolution although we rarely think about it. We take many cultural aspects of our lives for granted (such as the food we eat, the language we speak, the festivals we celebrate, the family traditions we continue, the way we dress, the music we listen to – the list is endless). However, if you had to describe yourself as a 'cultural being', that is, a product of culture, how would you do it?

Some people find it easier than others to decide what culture means to them and what aspects of their lives are culturally significant. Many years ago, I took a group of Asian young women (including Hindus, Muslims and Sikhs) to an inter-faith young women's residential. One of the exercises involved the young women being put into mixed inter-faith groups to discuss an object that they had brought with them and that they felt represented their cultural and/or religious background. I found it very striking that the Asian and African Caribbean girls found the exercise much easier, while the white European young women really struggled.

It was interesting to observe the ease with which the Asian girls produced clothing, jewellery and ornaments which consisted of religious symbols such as the Hindu *om* or the *trishul* (a spear with three points carried by Lord Shiva), the Sikh *kara* (metal bangle) or the *hijab* (scarf worn by Muslim girls and women), and the African Caribbean girls produced music such as reggae, poetry (in patois) and crucifixes (both carved in wood and worn as pendants with necklaces) or typical fruits from the Caribbean (such as mangoes and sugarcane).

The white European girls seemed lost, and their struggles to think about the symbolic representations of their culture led to the realisation that it was more difficult for them to do so for two reasons. Firstly, they never really had to think about it – they were in the majority and therefore part of that majority group in society that defined what was considered 'normal', that is 'the norm'. Secondly, they lived in a multicultural society where their lifestyles were influenced heavily by cultural symbols from elsewhere, especially in regard to their fashion and music sense. Even the food that they enjoyed seemed to be from 'elsewhere'. (There was a long discussion about how chicken tikka masala had become a favourite.)

The following group exercise will help you understand how important culture and the symbolic representations of culture can be in our lives.

ACTIVITY **1.4**

Individually and then in small groups (of no more than five people) imagine that you are in conflict with another group or community. You have been told that in order to coexist, you have to negotiate and decide what you are prepared to give up (and the other group or community is expected to do the same) from the following:

- *Your language*
- *Your national anthem*
- *Your country's flag*

ACTIVITY **1.4** *continued*

- *Your way of dress*
- *Your cuisine*

Decide which two things from the above you would be willing to give up and therefore go armed with this to the negotiations with representatives from the other group/community.

Remember that in your group you have to agree what is meant by each of the categories above before you decide to give them up as a group (for the negotiations). For example, what is meant by 'the flag' – is it the St George's flag, is it the Union Jack or is it the Welsh Dragon, etc?

When I have done this exercise with students, they have struggled to agree, both on how each of the categories is defined and what they would be prepared to give up as a group. Things become particularly fraught and tense in groups where the members come from diverse racial, cultural, religious and national backgrounds. What becomes clear is that feelings about these symbolic representations of their cultural identity run very deep. Culture resides in the minds and hearts of people.

Culture is shared between people and therefore a social phenomenon which makes it very important. The fact that meanings assigned to particular symbols (such as a flag) or to particular actions (such as a handshake) are understood collectively means that culture inevitably operates in the public arena and among particular groups who share an understanding of the meanings attached to particular actions and symbols. In short, culture exists in a context which is specific to particular groups of people with a shared history and therefore often a shared identity. The idea of sharing culturally specific behaviour and transmitting it from one generation to the next can give rise to what we call 'cultural traditions'. These in turn help to bridge our past and present actions and to connect us to wider society and often give rise to feelings of nostalgia. For example, how you celebrate Christmas or Eid or Diwali each year in your family may have resonance with how it was celebrated years earlier by your parents when they were children. So, there may be 'special' activities associated with the celebrations that are particular to your family, and yet the festivals listed above are clearly also celebrated by large numbers of people who are not in your family. Traditions are, therefore, important in all our lives and are the means by which we connect both with our pasts and with other people.

ACTIVITY **1.5**

- *Think about the traditions that you feel are important to you and why.*
- *If possible, discuss these with another person.*

However, traditions can also be shrouded in mystique, and often we may join in with them, without having any understanding of where they have come from and why they exist. They have a powerful hold over us.

Read the story below and think about what it shows about the notion of 'tradition.'

On Sundays, Alice did a roast with all the trimmings. However, before she put the joint of meat in the oven, she always cut it into half and then placed the two halves into the oven.

One day, her little son asked her why she always cut the joint of meat into two. Alice thought about it and then finally said, 'Well my mum always did so I do it too. We always have'.

So the next time that Alice saw her own mother, she asked her why they always cut the joint of meat into two halves. Alice's mother also said the same to her: 'Well, my mum always did, so I did too'.

As it happened, Alice's grandmother, although frail, was still alive. So when she next saw her, Alice asked her grandmother the same question, and her grandmother said: 'Well, in the old days, the ovens were always too small, so you couldn't cook it all unless you cut it into two halves.'

If you were in Alice's position, would you continue with her family tradition of cutting the joint into two?

The fact that cultural meanings are shared between people is significant and leads to what Geertz (1973 cited in Inglis, 2000, page 12) describes as the distinction between 'thin' and 'thick' descriptions of culture. For example, although a wink and a twitch of the eye may be phenomenological and therefore the same physical eye movement, they have very different significance because of the context. Therefore, in our society, when you wink at somebody, you are conveying a particular message to that person, which is understood by others – it is a deliberate action. A deliberate wink, therefore, has a particular meaning which is culturally specific. This is an example of a 'thick' description of culture. However, a twitch of the eye is just that, and nothing more, and therefore that is generally what would be described as a 'thin' description of culture.

The relationship between culture and ethnicity and culture and national identity is an interesting one. The relationship between culture and ethnicity is significant because ethnicity depends on culture but is not constrained by it. An example of this could be the Irish community (as a cultural group) who live in both Northern and Southern Ireland (Eire) – there may be a great sharing of culture between the two in spite of potential differences in religion and nationality (which demonstrates how culture can cross the boundaries potentially posed by religion and nationality).

With regard to the relationship between culture and national identity, this crossing and fusing of boundaries becomes just as apparent. The development of nation states has had an influence on culture as people often describe themselves in terms of their national identity (such as Pakistani, Indian, Jamaican, Irish), which demonstrates that culture can be and has been influenced by the formation of the nation states and that it can have a political aspect when it is linked to national identity. However, cultural traditions and behaviour often pre-date the development of the nation state – for example, Punjabi is spoken by the Punjabi communities in both India and Pakistan, although communities from the two countries may often choose to define themselves by their national identity rather than their cultural, linguistic one. Although the two communities from the two different countries may have a lot in common culturally, they may still wish to distinguish themselves from each other by virtue of their different national identities, which are steeped in the history and politics of the Indian subcontinent.

Culture, therefore, is an important aspect of our individual identity and is also the means by which we often connect with others who we think and feel are culturally similar to us. This ability of culture to be important both on a personal and a group level makes it a dynamic force. In short, it can help an individual to answer the question 'Who and what am I?' while at the same time helping define our sense of belonging to groups and wider communities of people, so that it also helps us think about who and what we are. It is an evolving force which can change the way an individual and community behaves from one generation to the next, while retaining enough of a resonance with the past for the connections between past and present to be significant. It is this complex and dynamic aspect of culture which makes it both exciting and bewildering.

C H A P T E R   R E V I E W

This chapter explored the significance of and the influences encountered by individuals in the shaping of their identity. It also examined the importance of self-awareness (in relation to one's identity) in youth and community work practice. The concept of culture was also explored, as was the relationship between identity and culture.

FURTHER READING

Weedon, C (2004) *Identity and Culture: Narratives of Difference and Belonging.* Maidenhead: Open University Press.

This is an interesting text which explores both identity and culture and the relationship between them. Using examples from history, politics, fiction and the visual, Weedon examines social power relations that create subject positions and forms of individual and group identities in multiethnic, postcolonial societies.

Woodward, K (ed.) (2007) *Identity and Difference*. London: Sage.

This is a very useful text that explores identity and difference. Sections 2 (Why Does the Concept of Identity Matter?) and 4 (How is Difference Marked in Relation to Identity) are especially relevant.

Chapter 2
De-mystifying some concepts

Introduction

This chapter explores the often confusing language associated with cross-cultural dynamics. It first discusses what is meant by the terms 'cross-', 'inter-' and 'intra-cultural' and then explores some of the language and concepts related to these, such as the notions of 'race', 'ethnicity' and 'nationality' and the relationships between them, and also their relationship to the concept of culture.

Inter-/cross- and intra-cultural

In his discussion on culture, Cashmore (1988, page 69) suggests that

Cultures tend to be systems of meaning and custom that are blurred at the edges. Nor are they normally stable. As individuals come to terms with changing circumstances (such as new technology) so they change their ways and shared meanings change with them.

Although Cashmore cites the influence of technology as a force for potential change, I think that the 'territory' within which different cultures encounter each other is also an important force for evolution and change. Therefore, in the milieu of a multi-cultural society, such as that of Britain, it is inevitable that people from different cultures will come across each other, and in the process, be both influenced by each other and reflect on the differences and similarities between them. I think that this process of cross-cultural or inter-cultural encounters or dynamics is fascinating, challenging, confusing and sometimes even daunting.

Indeed, the language associated with it can be potentially just as confusing as the encounters themselves. This is a good time to address some of the points that cause confusion, starting with the terminology.

An online search (Cambridge Dictionaries Online, 2011) for the meaning of the prefixes inter- and cross-, which are often attached to the term 'cultural' (i.e., 'cross-cultural' and 'inter-cultural'), produced the following:

> *Cross- (prefix)*
>
> *across*
>
> *including different groups or subjects*

and

> *Inter- (prefix)*
>
> *used to form adjectives meaning between or among the stated people, things or places.*

These definitions suggest that there is little difference in the meanings attached to the prefixes 'cross-' and 'inter-', and therefore, as Knapp and Knapp-Potthoff (1987, page 7) suggest, the term 'cross-cultural' is often used synonymously with 'inter-cultural'.

According to an analytical research process the prefix 'cross-' can be applied or used and that is, perhaps, the source of the confusion. As Knapp and Knapp-Potthoff (1987, page 7) further clarify:

> *Traditionally, 'cross-', as in 'cross-linguistic' or 'cross-check' implies a comparison of phenomena. Therefore, the adequate use of 'cross-cultural' depends on the analyst's perspective: if different cultures are to be compared with respect to the occurrence of, for example a certain form of language use, the approach is 'cross-cultural', but if the focus is an ongoing interaction among members of different (sub-)cultures, 'intercultural' communication is at issue.*

In relation to youth and community work practice, both inter- and cross-cultural dynamics are used interchangeably and usually refer to the more recently coined idea of 'working with diversity'.

To add to the possible confusion, the prefix 'intra-' is also used before the term 'cultural', and in this case, the prefix means 'within' or 'inside' (Collins, 1998, page 805). Many of us will have encountered this prefix, for example, in relation to the word intravenous or in an organisational context referring to the intranet, which is the internal electronic communication system within an organisation. Intra-cultural, therefore, refers to the differences and variations that exist within a particular culture. For example, although African-Caribbean people in Britain may often be regarded as a homogenous entity, the fact is that members of the African-Caribbean community in Britain originate from the different islands in the Caribbean, all with their distinct histories, and therefore, ensuing traditions, language, cuisine and other cultural aspects.

The territory within which cultures encounter each other, as I have already suggested, can be exciting yet confusing, but in relation to practice, it can also be an arena which is fraught and has the potential to spark conflict if the worker is not alert to the complexity of the interactions. Reflections on my practice in multi-cultural settings and especially in relation to international youth exchanges that I have been involved in have identified culinary and hospitality practices and inter-cultural communication as two areas that can be especially problematic.

For example, when planning a self-catering residential with multi-cultural groups of young people, I remember having lengthy discussions with the group about ensuring 'cultural sensitivity' in relation to shopping for food and preparation of meals. Apart from limiting the costs, the residentials were ideal not only for teaching life skills and teamwork but also for raising awareness of the different religious and cultural practices represented in the group, and the importance of respecting these differences in practice. Thus, often the 'planned' meals would exclude pork and beef because of the Rastafarians, Muslims, Hindus and Sikhs in the group. It would also always mean that vegetarian food was done completely separately, including the use of utensils (which had to be kept completely separate for each of the dishes to avoid the 'contamination' of the vegetarian food with utensils used to stir or serve a meat-based dish). The reasons for the meticulous planning were not only about respecting differences, and ensuring that individuals in the group felt included, accepted and valued, but also about avoiding conflict between group members because they felt angry about being disrespected on religious and/or cultural grounds.

When I was involved in a youth exchange between a multi-cultural group of young people from Birmingham and Barcelona, the discussions about what individuals would or could eat and how the food should be prepared took the most time to clarify.

ACTIVITY **2.1**

This activity can be undertaken individually or in a small group.

Imagine that you are in the process of planning an international youth exchange to Jamaica. The worker from your partner group in Jamaica is a Rastafarian and is visiting your organisation as part of an Advanced Planning Visit, before the youth group arrives in Britain for the first leg of the exchange. You need to host your visitor for a few days and plan the itinerary for the Jamaican group's visit in a few months. Think about what you need to know about your visitor's cultural and religious practices to ensure that you host him or her in a culturally sensitive or culturally appropriate way.

*

This activity can also be undertaken individually or in a small group.

Reflect on the complexity of the interaction about knowledge and understanding demonstrated in the following scenario.

Years ago, I visited the home of an older Muslim Pakistani woman and her family. As is customary in such encounters, I was offered snacks and drinks. As the teenage daughter brought out a plate of pakoras, onion bhajis and samosas, the mother said,

> *Don't worry, I know you are a Hindu and a vegetarian. The samosas and pakoras are vegetarian, and I made sure I fried them in fresh, newly opened vegetable oil, and used a ladle which has been washed and cleaned. They're not fried in oil I have used for kebabs.*

I often wonder whether she was just very culturally aware or whether I had given any signs of looking anxious about deciding whether to accept or politely decline the hospitality offered.

The aforementioned activities are important to help you consider the potential complexities, knowledge and understanding needed to work in a culturally diverse context, and particularly make you think about inter- and intra-cultural dynamics. The two examples above tend to focus on the domain of culinary and hospitality experiences, which can be the source of much disenchantment between people if the worker is not alert to the potential differences between individuals and groups that he or she works with. Inter-cultural communication can be just as problematic and a potential for real confusion and misunderstanding.

A few simple examples from my own international youth exchange work can demonstrate this. When I was liaising with professionals in India and in Germany on separate exchanges, I was struck by their use of the word 'animator' or 'animateur'. It took me a while to realise that, in fact, this was a reference to what I would commonly describe as a 'worker' or 'practitioner'. The idea of a 'workshop' in an Indian context is much less interactive than I would expect it to be in Britain. These two examples illustrate how different words can be used for particular concepts in different countries and how the same word can have slightly different connotations and expectations attached to it.

A final example concerns the common use of language in one country in a way that is completely unexpected, but which is founded on the logical application of rules within a language. Having taken a youth group to the city of Madurai in South India as part of the first leg of a youth exchange, the group realised that the train tickets that our hosts had booked were actually for a date that was a little later than expected and that, in fact, the group needed to leave Madurai for Chennai one day before the date stated on the tickets. Having realised this, I went to the station to get the date changed. As I approached the ticket kiosk (conscious of a growing queue behind me) and explained to the ticket seller that the group needed to leave Madurai a day earlier than stated on the tickets, she asked, "So Ma'am you want to pre-pone these tickets?"

I asked her to repeat what she had said three times, not really understanding the question, and was conscious of the growing frustration behind me in the queue. After a while, I worked it out, she was applying the prefix 'pre' to 'pone', which is the second part of 'post-pone'. Of course it was completely logical and all the Indians that I spoke to afterwards did not seem to appreciate my confusion or lack of understanding; the term 'pre-pone' was commonly used, accepted and understood to mean 'bringing something forward' in India. They were unaware and unconcerned that it was not used at all in Britain.

Therefore the use of a common language between different cultural groups can also be a source of misunderstanding, and the terms used and the respective understanding of them need to be clarified and reflected on to try and minimise the potential for the misunderstandings.

Other concepts – race, class, ethnicity and nationality

A textbook on cross-cultural dynamics in relation to youth and community work practice cannot be complete without some exploration of the concept of 'race'. This is particularly significant in the context of Britain being a multi-racial/multi-cultural society, with a growing mixed race or dual-heritage population. Significantly, in 2003, Granada (the television broadcasting company) produced a *Cultural Diversity Guide*, which included a section on mixed race. It points out that

> *The inclusion of a section on 'mixed race' in a Cultural Diversity Guide illustrates the reality of contemporary British society in both positive and negative ways. In positive terms it highlights the diversity of the British population and the fact that relationships are formed across racialised boundaries. In negative terms, it indicates that divisions still exist between groups classified as discrete 'races' on the basis of physical characteristics* (Johnson, page 151).

The aforementioned quote suggests that 'race' is generally concerned with the differences in relation to physical characteristics. Knapp and Knapp-Potthoff (1987, page 6) simply suggest,

> *What makes the notion of race easier to handle than that of culture is the fact that 'race' can be more clearly defined: a race is usually considered as a group of people who have certain biological features in common.*

However, it is important to note that in spite of the visible differences in phenotype (the actual differences in skin colour), there is no scientific basis for the concept of 'race'.

The actual word 'race' can be traced in the English language to the sixteenth century, and until the nineteenth century it referred to common biological features present because of shared descent. However, in more recent times the term has had to be defined differently, especially concerning social purposes and contexts. For social scientists, it has become correlated with

a group of people who are **socially** *defined in a given society as belonging together because of* **physical markers** *such as skin pigmentation, hair texture, facial features, stature and the like.*

(Cashmore, 1988, page 238)

What is important to remember, given the fact that 'race' is meaningless in scientific terms, is that the concept is a social or political construct (Fryer, 1984), which, in turn, is associated with issues and positions of relative power and influence in particular societies such as British society. This, in turn, gives rise to the notion of racism, which is simply described in the *Cultural Diversity Guide* (Johnson, 2003, page 156) as 'the belief that discrimination against a person on the basis of race or ethnic grouping is justified'.

It is the concept of 'class' that is usually related to notions about position, status and relative wealth and power in a society. The Collins English Dictionary provides a good summary of meanings associated with a generally quite contested, widely discussed concept.

1. a collection or division of people or things sharing a common characteristic, attribute, quality or property;

2. a group of persons sharing a similar social position and certain economic, political and cultural characteristics;

3. (in Marxist theory) a group or persons sharing the same relationship to the means of production;

4a. the pattern of divisions that exist within a society on the basis of rank, economic status, etc;

4b. (as modifier): the class struggle; class distinctions.

(Collins English Dictionary, 1998, page 298)

The fact is that class also has a way of 'grouping' people, and this is often combined with a sense of belonging that those grouped together may feel. This, in turn, may mean that there is also a sense of shared identity and, therefore, a shared culture between people who perhaps feel that they belong to similar strata of society. Meighan and Harber, for example, point out that:

Subjectively social class raises other problems of definition. Various national opinion polls have shown that people accept the existence of different social classes, will assign themselves to upper, middle or working classes, and think that the major factor in judging position is accent, occupation, money or education.

(Meighan and Harber, 2007, page 390)

Significantly, class can and does clearly intersect with race and other aspects of collective identity, so that in every racial group or community in a multi-racial society, you would expect to find people who are assigned an identity based on both their class and race.

The youth and community practitioners' awareness of the legislation and policies (such as the Race Relations Act of 1976; the Race Amendment Act of 2000; Equal Opportunities Policy) being in existence and the implementation of these policies necessary to challenge racism and minimise its effects on British society is essential, but is not the focus of this textbook. The focus here is just on de-mystifying the language associated with inter- or cross-cultural dynamics.

Therefore, just like the notion of culture, the concept of ethnicity is bandied about and contested. In fact, Ratcliffe (2004, page 28) refers to it as a 'highly contested terrain'.

I think that the origin of the term 'ethnicity' is significant as it is rooted in the Latin word 'ethnicus', which means 'heathen'. Concerning these early origins, it is related to notions and people who were not Christian or Jewish. Its early usage was associated with labelling a group as being different, and more significantly, as having lesser status.

More recently, Ratcliffe (2004, page 28) suggests that the term 'ethnicity' is deployed loosely to imply commonalities of language, religion, identity, national origins and/ or even skin colour. In short, for Ratcliffe it seems to have more to do with the situation or context encountered by a particular population. In relation to this, Bulmer (1986, page 54) suggests that it is to do with memories of a shared past and therefore a 'collective memory of people'. However, memories can be contested, and it is not always clear whether they are based on historical facts, and even if they were, whose or which version of history should they be based on. For example, clearly the history of white settlement in South Africa will read very differently depending on whether you read the African National Congress (ANC) version or the version written by the white Boer settlers. Closer to home, I have often had to referee a raging debate between students about whether the Handsworth riots in Birmingham in the 1980s were an example of an 'uprising' or just 'anti-social behaviour'. Depending on the individual perspectives present in the debate, the events clearly had very different connotations for the students involved in the debate.

However in spite of these complexities the term ethnic is in vogue and as Knapp and Knapp-Potthoff (1987, page 6) point out,

The term has become popular in Britain and the USA above all in combinations like 'ethnic identity', 'ethnic food', 'ethnic bookshop' etc. 'The use of these

expressions points to the fact that the term 'ethnic' is preferred for describing groups of minorities living in the same geographical area as the majority population, rather than for characterising groups of people living in different countries, say Japanese people living in Japan in contrast to Frenchmen living in France. The very fact that the term 'ethnic' and its derivations are mainly used for groups living in a 'multi-ethnic' society is connected with the emphasis on 'boundaries' and 'differences' in definitions of 'ethnic' and 'ethnicity'.

Again, for the youth and community work practitioner, the need to work with diversity means having an understanding of how minorities, both ethnic and cultural, are situated and how they relate to the majority population. More importantly, it is about appreciating the boundaries, similarities and differences between groups, which are present in the local practice-related setting and in the nation as a whole.

If the focus of ethnicity is shared experiences and group- or community-wide memories of such experiences (Knapp and Knapp-Potthoff, 1987; Ratcliffe, 2004), then the practitioner needs to make some effort to research and understand the 'stories' related to the diverse minorities or communities present in both the geographical location in which the practice is based and in relation to the minorities present within the country as a whole.

ACTIVITY **2.3**

This activity can be undertaken individually or in small groups which can encourage deeper discussion and understanding.

Think of someone you know, who is ethnically different from you, and make a note of the perceived differences between you and this other person. How you have become aware of these differences? What questions, if any, you would like to ask this person about his or her ethnic identity?

The aforementioned activity is just meant to provide some food for thought, because it can help facilitate reflection on your perception of differences and enable you to acknowledge how much or how little you know about these and whether you would be comfortable or confident to ask the questions that you would like to explore to get a better understanding.

Often, the boundaries between people who are ethnically different from each other are fraught with feelings of uncertainty, and sentiments such as 'I don't want to offend anybody', 'I don't want to appear ignorant', 'I'm not sure who to ask'.

I believe that the concept of the 'nation' is the final piece of the complex puzzle, which contributes to the general sense of confusion and sometimes lack of knowledge and understanding that youth and community workers may experience when working especially, although not exclusively, in ethnically and culturally diverse settings. The sense of allegiance to a particular nation can also be a very fraught idea, which can give rise to powerful sentiments and emotions. For example, I remember some of my students becoming very agitated when I revealed to them that as a cricket fan, I supported India against England whenever the two teams played. They were understandably annoyed and bewildered by my support for the Indian cricket team, when I had grown up and gone to school in England, had never lived in India and was proud to have British nationality. It was and is confusing for me to explain the idea of how we make sense of the many communities to which we belong. More specifically, among the many communities for each of which we nurture a sense of belonging is the idea of 'imagined community' (Anderson, 1983, page 49), which suggests that we have sentimental links to communities that we *imagine* we belong to. Therefore, as someone who is ethnically Indian, I cannot help but become sentimental about other members of my *imagined* community, and this is brought into sharp focus for me when England plays cricket against India.

Allegiance to a nation gives rise to the concept of 'nationalism', which Cashmore (1988, pages 204–205) explains as the following:

> *As an ideology, nationalism contains three main ideas. First, it argues that an identified population should be able to formulate institutions and laws with which to determine its own future. Second, it maintains that each such population has a unique set of characteristics which identify it as a 'nation'. Third, and consequently, it claims that the world is divided naturally into a number of such distinct 'nations'. This combination of ideas and claims constitute the basis for political strategies and movements which, since the nineteenth century, have had a major influence on the way in which the world is organised politically.*

Thus, in reality, national boundaries generally decide where one country ends or borders another. These boundaries are often the result of historical and often tumultuous wars of liberation and negotiation which are now established (although there are still exceptions to this) and therefore define the political organisation of the world. Often, and especially in relation to the ethnic groups and communities settled in Britain, there are historical ties which can be traced, for example, to the British Empire. So, it is not surprising that there are communities settled in Britain originating from the former British colonies, including from the Caribbean and the Indian sub-continent, which are now nations in their own right (such as Jamaica, India, Pakistan, Bangladesh). Some of these nations allow citizens to have dual nationality, while others may not. Therefore, people of a Pakistani origin, for example, are currently entitled to hold dual nationality and therefore be citizens of both Britain and Pakistan, whereas the Indian government does not allow this.

To add to the complexity, social scientists often refer to the notion of 'Diaspora', which in current times refers to 'dispersion or spreading of people originally belonging to one nation or having a common culture' (Collins, 1998, page 433). Therefore, the Pakistani community in Britain also belongs to the Pakistani Diaspora, which includes all the communities originating from Pakistan and now settled around the world.

The inter-play between nationality, ethnicity and culture is fascinating, since the idea of the nation-state is 'new' in relation to how the world is organised. The fact is that ethnicity and culture can often pre-date the sense of national identity and so, for example, an Indian Punjabi (from the Punjab region in India) and a Pakistani Punjabi (from the Punjab region in Pakistan) may have a lot in common with each other, including the language and culinary habits and yet be completely distinct in terms of their national origin. The example of the Punjabis is an interesting case, since the British government was historically involved in the forging of the boundaries between Pakistan and India in 1947, which involved the splitting of the state of Punjab between the two new nations formed at that time. This resulted in thousands of people losing their lives as Hindus and Sikhs moved out of Pakistani Punjab to the Indian side and the Muslims did the same leaving India and moving to the Pakistani side. The 'hangover' in terms of the strength of feelings regarding this fraught event still has a resonance for the communities settled in Britain from the two 'parts' of the Punjab, originating from the two distinct nations.

CASE STUDY: BILAL'S STORY

Bilal was born in 1935 in the Indian province of East Bengal, which between 1757 and 1947 was part of British India. In 1947, as a result of the partition between India and Pakistan, the province became a part of East Pakistan. Then, during a period of bloody unrest and the great flood of 1970, East Bengal split from Pakistan and became a part of the Republic of Bangladesh in 1971. In 1972 Bilal left Bangladesh for Britain and has been living in the East End of London ever since. He visits Bangladesh often, because his extended family is split between Britain and Bangladesh. He is a British national now.

Reflection on Bilal's story demonstrates that although he has remained racially, culturally and ethnically the same, his national identity has, in fact, changed a number of times. No wonder working with diversity and understanding the complexity of race, ethnicity, culture and nationality is complex and sometimes daunting for the practitioner. However, 'unpacking' this complexity can be fascinating and often people will readily welcome the opportunity to share their experiences – if only they are asked in the right manner.

Unfortunately it is not as simple as that, since in Britain Myers and Grosvenor (2001, page 253) suggest that:

The idea of the nation has, in other words, always been used as an instrument of government to identify those who belong, those who are like 'us', and those who are different, a threat and therefore who must be excluded.

The sense of 'where and to which group of people do I belong?' can be difficult for the individual who is racially, ethnically and culturally different from others around him or her, and sentiments attached to national identity make the situation even more complex. The power to include and exclude individuals and groups in a society has an inevitable political dimension, which those in any position of authority have to understand. Therefore, my support and allegiance to the Indian cricket team can very easily play into the hands of those who, unfortunately, do not understand or are simply not interested in understanding the complexity involved in discovering why I may feel the way that I do. The role of the youth and community practitioner is to be interested, to listen to the stories of difference and commonalities around them and to develop an understanding in themselves and help forge it in others, if possible.

ACTIVITY 2.4

The final activity in this chapter aims to gauge the extent to which you have understood the concepts discussed in this chapter.

Complete each of the sentences below by choosing a word/phrase/concept from the box below.

Inter-cultural	Racism	Race
Ethnicity		
	Nationality	
Nation-state	Intra-cultural	

1. _____ relates to the differences and variations within a particular ethnic group.

2. Prejudice on the basis of racial differences is known as _____.

3. _____ is a contested concept that relates to differences in phenotype and is also considered to be a social construct.

4. A _____ is the political organisation of a sovereign entity or country as a territorial unit.

5. The contested concept of _____ relates to commonalities of religion, identity, language, national origins and/or race.

6. An individual's _____ gives that person membership, and/or citizenship of a nation state or sovereign state.

7. _____ relates to the dynamics between individuals and groups belonging to different cultures.

C H A P T E R   R E V I E W

This chapter focused on the confusing language concerned with working with diversity and/or cross-cultural dynamics. I hope that the activities helped you to reflect on the fascinating nature of the boundaries and encounters between people who are racially, ethnically and culturally diverse and originate from many different nations, but with whom you work as a youth and community worker in Britain.

FURTHER READING

Imam, UF (1999) Youth workers as mediators and interpreters, in Banks, S (ed.) *Ethical Issues in Youth Work*. London: Routledge.

This is an interesting chapter that explores the complex, ethically challenging position that youth workers find themselves in when working with Black young people growing up within multi-ethnic social frameworks (page 125).

Kim, YY (2003) Adapting to an unfamiliar culture: An interdisciplinary overview, in Gudykunst, WB (ed) *Cross-Cultural and Intercultural Communication*. London: Sage.

This chapter explores the impact of being immersed in an unfamiliar culture and includes discussion about the process of short-term and long-term adaptation.

Ratcliffe, P (2004) *Race, Ethnicity and Difference: Imagining the Inclusive Society*. Maidenhead: Open University Press.

This book explores the social significance attached to various forms of difference, especially race and ethnicity. The third chapter on 'Ethnicity, Culture and Difference' is particularly useful.

Chapter 3

Some concepts and theories

Introduction

As the focus of the last chapter was to demystify some of the terminology associated with cross-cultural dynamics, the aim of this chapter is to discuss some of the concepts and theories significant for understanding and working with diversity, especially when such dynamics are often closely linked to understanding the impact and interplay of power and authority in relation to the different cultural communities in any multi-cultural society.

Therefore, the discussion will begin by focusing on the concept of oppression, the principles of equity and equality and then a number of theories including some that would help explain particular tendencies and prejudiced attitudes in relation to the 'other', such as the theories of Orientalism (Said, 1978), 'closed' and 'open' views of 'the other' (Parekh, 2000) and hegemony (Gramsci, 1971). These are important for providing a way of understanding relative position and authority of respective individuals, groups and communities in any society.

Oppression

One of the main definitions of the verb 'to oppress' is 'to subjugate by cruelty, force, etc.' and 'to afflict or torment' (Collins, 1998, page 1092). Therefore, oppression is the act of oppressing. The interesting thing about oppression is the fact that it includes within it both the act of being oppressive and the state of being oppressed. So, both the oppressing and the oppressed are intrinsically implicated within the concept. The origins of the concept emanate from the Latin word 'opprimere', which means to press against (Collins, 1998, page 1092).

The 'classical' or 'traditional' understanding of the concept of oppression tends to conjure up an idea of injustice, tyranny or cruelty which is overt and often considered in a historical and distant way. Classical examples may, therefore, include the slave trade and/or connotations of conquest such as the colonial domination of other societies. This 'classical' interpretation of oppression can mean that in the present day, living in a democratic society, there may be a tendency to distance ourselves from it and to think that oppression is somewhere else or took place in the past and because we live in an enlightened civilised society, it does not or cannot have a hold in our society.

However, as Young (1990, page 41) suggests, contemporary understandings of the concept are important for explaining disadvantage in societies. Young states that the concept designates as, '…some people suffer disadvantage and injustice not because of 'tyrannical power', but because of the everyday practices of a well-intentional liberal society'.

Therefore, a contemporary understanding of oppression infers that it is systematic, structural and embedded in the norms, habitual processes and symbols of a society. In some senses, this can be viewed almost as oppression without an overt oppressor, as the established structures and processes can be responsible for the systematic oppression of particular individuals and groups within a society.

Young (1990) in fact suggests that there are five 'faces of oppression', each is important to consider and reflect on to develop contemporary understanding of the concept. The first of the five faces is 'exploitation', which is the process of transferring the fruits of the efforts or labours of one social group or individual to benefit another.

A prominent tragic example is the death of 18 Chinese cockle-pickers in 2004 who were trapped by the rising tide at Morecambe Bay (Watts, 2007). As the tragic events unfolded, it transpired that most of them were illegal migrant workers from China, exploited by others to work for little or nothing.

ACTIVITY **3.1**

Consider the following questions and, if possible, discuss your responses with a small group.

- *Can you think of another contemporary example of this process?*
- *How do or can people who are exploited respond?*

Young (1990) describes the second face of oppression as 'marginalisation', which is the process by which an individual or group is forced into the periphery of society, usually by virtue of the fact that they are members of a group that the society cannot or will not use. The preceding example of the illegal migrant workers lends itself well to this definition of marginalisation. The process (of marginalisation) can be both overt or explicit (as in the example above), and more subtle and covert. For example, I remember being asked in an interview for a post as a youth worker, whether, given my identity as an Asian woman, I would be able to work at unsociable hours. The experience left me feeling angry and bewildered, but it demonstrated how the process of marginalisation is steeped in assumptions and stereotypes expressed, as in this case, by well-meaning individuals.

ACTIVITY **3.2**

Consider the following questions, and if possible, discuss your responses with a small group.

- *Have you ever felt marginalised? When and why?*
- *How did you respond?*

The third face of oppression is 'powerlessness'. This involves an individual or group lacking authority or the ability to mediate the decisions of others (especially those in power). Powerlessness can mean having power without being able to exercise it yourself, and therefore having to take orders without having the right to give them. It can also mean having little opportunity to develop and exercise ideas and skills that you might have (Young, 1990). The sense of being powerless can be frustrating, and can affect individuals in particular situations, as well as whole groups of people and communities within societies. The notion of having a voice or being silent and/or silenced is an aspect of belonging to a group which feels powerless.

ACTIVITY **3.3**

Consider the following questions and, if possible, discuss your responses with a small group.

- *Can you think of a situation where you felt powerless?*
- *What did you do and how did you feel?*
- *How did others react to you or perceive you?*

The fourth face of oppression, according to Young's (1990) model for understanding oppression, is 'cultural imperialism'. This is closely linked to individuals and groups in a society feeling powerless and therefore lacking the ability and/or opportunity to establish the meanings attached to norms within a society. As a result the dominant meanings within a society make your own group's perspective invisible, and in fact reduce them to caricature and stereotypes. I remember listening to an older Welsh colleague some years ago as she described the punishment she experienced as a child at school when she was caught speaking in Welsh. She said that children who made such a 'mistake' were made to wear a cardboard sign for the whole day with the word 'Welsh' on it. This is an extreme example of cultural imperialism related to the preservation of English as the most important, significant and prevalent language within the land.

In terms of my own experiences in relation to this, the idea in Western societies that eye-contact portrays a sense of earnestness has been a real issue for me as an Asian woman. I have had to really learn to 'hold' eye contact with friends and colleagues who are not Asian, even the men! Although this may sound comical, the significance of such a symbolic act as 'having eye-contact' is at the heart of some of the contentious debates in present-day multi-cultural societies, and in particular, at the centre of the issue of whether Muslim women should be allowed to wear the veil or 'niqab' in public spaces. Both sides to this debate are steeped in cultural imperialism.

ACTIVITY **3.4**

At the heart of the notion of cultural imperialism is the raging debate which is summarised by how you would respond to the old adage – 'When in Rome, do as the Romans do'. Therefore, think about it and, if possible, discuss your responses to the following questions.

- *In a multi-cultural society, should everyone be treated the same or should different cultural needs be addressed and encouraged to flourish?*
- *What would your expectations be in relation to this if you were to migrate to a country with a completely different culture?*

The fifth and final face of oppression is perhaps the most obvious, because it is overt. It is 'violence' which targets, through unprovoked attacks humiliation, intimidation, stigmatisation or harassment, members of a certain social group. The unprovoked attack on and death of Stephen Lawrence in April 1993 is a good example of this (Lawrence, 2009).

ACTIVITY **3.5**

Think about it and (if possible) discuss the following questions.

- *What other manifestations of oppression as violence can you think of?*
- *How do you think the fear of violence can affect an individual's or group's health and well being?*

The five faces of oppression, presented by Young (1990), is a comprehensive model and is important for youth and community workers to recognise and understand in relation to their own lives, especially in relation to the individuals, groups and communities with and within which they work. Youth and community practitioners are often catalysts for change, especially in situations of powerlessness, but this can only happen if there is an understanding of the experience of oppression.

Equality and equity

The idea of equality of opportunity is enshrined by legislative framework within British society, and requires organisations to implement equal opportunity policies. For youth and community workers the principle of equality of opportunity underpins all practice and is considered as important as the other principles of participation, education and empowerment.

However, as Cashmore (1988, page 93) states, 'There are a bewildering number of senses in which this concept can be used, but uniting them all is the assertion that, in all public matter, humans should be both treated identically and given exactly the same degree of access to scarce resources'.

Most people interpret this as a tendency towards the concept of fairness. Yet the notion of being 'fair' can be very problematic. For example, how fair are my actions as a youth worker if I have the means to take a group swimming for free and let all the interested young people know and put up a poster proclaiming that everyone would be welcome and all those interested are to meet at 6 p.m. on a Friday evening at the Youth Centre. I find on the evening that of the 12 young people that turn up, all are either white or African Caribbean and 10 of the 12 are young men in spite of my centre being in a multi-cultural setting. On the surface, I think I have been fair in this scenario, but I am conscious that not many of the young women had come along, and certainly I had no representatives from among any Asian young people. So, in earnest, how fair have I been? Certainly in regard to equality of opportunity I think I have been very 'fair'; everybody had been told, and even a poster was put up telling young people, those interested, to meet at 6 p.m. on Friday evening.

The scenario exemplifies the tension between fairness in providing an opportunity and the actual fairness in relation to an outcome. In this case, the outcome is that young people can go swimming for free, but the fact that mainly young men from particular cultural backgrounds come along belies a deeper issue regarding the *ability* or willingness to take advantage of the opportunity given the social circumstances that it is offered in by the worker.

This brings into play the notion of equity. The dictionary definition of equality suggests that it is simply 'The state of being equal' and that equity is 'the quality of being impartial or reasonable; fairness' or 'an impartial or fair act, decision, etc.' (Collins, 1998, page 522).

Thus, equity is concerned with the *process* by which real fairness can be achieved.

In short, it is concerned with the creation of a level playing field to correct social development.

The following exercise, adapted from a discussion on equality and equity in relation to social policy by Blakemore and Griggs (2007), helps to demonstrate the distinction between the two concepts.

SCENARIO 1

Consider what you would do in the following situation:

It is your birthday and you have invited a few of your friends along to share your birthday cake. Of the four friends you have invited, one has been to a corporate event and been 'wined and dined' throughout the day. The second managed to 'grab' a sandwich at lunch. The third had a 'hearty' breakfast first thing in the morning, but nothing else throughout the day. The fourth and last of the invited friends woke up late, hadn't had time for breakfast, and then things 'came up' so there was no time to get anything throughout the day.

How would you divide your birthday cake, given what you know about your friends and their 'day', by the time they get to you?

When I describe this scenario and inevitably pose the 'final' question to my students, on the whole most students are inclined to divide the cake equally, because they claim that this is fair, and all four friends are being treated 'the same', and therefore equally. In relation to the concepts of equality and equity, a concern for equity would mean that the cake is divided in such a way that the hungriest would be given the greatest share first, but this can be uncomfortable when it is important to be fair. However in professional practice it is important to go beyond what seems fair on the surface and actually understand the significance of real fairness, fairness in actual outcome, which should be defined by need. That is why in a youth centre, which is perhaps dominated by young men, it is important to challenge the status quo and establish a young women's club or young women's night, etc.

The next exercise makes a more clear link to a needs-based response, which exemplifies the importance of understanding the concept of equity.

SCENARIO 2

You've been invited to a meeting involving the allocation of new funds. Of the 10p available, you are told that the 'criteria' is that no one person can be given the same amount as another and that the 10p cannot be divided equally between the five young people you know would really benefit from the extra new funds. Think about all the young people you work with and consider how you would divide the 10p and why? How would you justify your way of dividing the new 10p in funds?

Orientalism

In 1978 Edward Said, a Palestinian by origin, published a ground-breaking piece of work entitled *Orientalism: Western Conceptions of the Orient*. This was a stinging critique of the power relations between the East and the West and an analysis of Western discourse and perceptions of the East. Through this work the concept or theory of Orientalism was established. In relation to cross-cultural dynamics, including relationships between individuals and groups which originate in a multi-cultural society, inevitably from both the communities of the East and of the West, the theory deserves some attention. As King (1999, page 83) states:

> *Indeed such has been the influence of Said's work in this arena that the term 'Orientalism' is often now used as a pejorative term denoting the colonial manipulation of the Orient in general.*

Orientalism consists of three inter-related phenomena. The first of the three relates to who can be deemed to be an Orientalist. For Said (1978) an Orientalist refers to any individual involved in researching, writing about or teaching about the Orient including its cultures. The second phenomenon relates to how such individuals think about the Orient in relation to the West or as Said (1978) describes it 'the Occident'. Said (1978, page 2) says, 'Orientalism is a style of thought based upon an ontological and epistemological distinction made between 'the Orient' and (most of the time) 'the Occident'.'

The third phenomenon describes the relationship between the Orient and the Occident in relation to the West having the power to describe and define the East. In Said's words:

> *Orientalism can be discussed and analysed as the corporate institution for dealing with the Orient – dealing with it by making statements about it, authorising views of it, describing it, teaching it, settling it, ruling over it.*

> (1978, page 3)

In relation to youth and community practice, especially when working in multi-cultural settings, including Asian and Middle-Eastern communities, the theory of Orientalism provides a basis for questioning existing assumptions and stereotypes about these communities. It is a useful reminder that people like to define themselves and not be understood or judged through the eyes of others – especially 'others' who are not like them. In short, they want an equal voice in any discourse about them. If there is to be true acceptance and not just tolerance between different individuals and communities, then both or all those involved in any conversation must have an equal voice and the chance to be able to define themselves in any discourse. Acceptance requires a degree of respect which is not always implicit in the notion of tolerance. However, as Said wonders:

> *The real issue is whether indeed there can be a true representation of anything or whether any and all representations, because they are representations,*

are embedded first in the language and then in the culture, institutions, and political ambience of the representer. If the latter alternative is the correct one ... then we must be prepared to accept the fact that a representation is eo ipso implicated, intertwined, embedded, interwoven with a great many other things besides the 'truth', which is itself a representation.

(1978, page 272)

ACTIVITY **3.6**

Think about what you know about cultures of the East, including those communities from the East that are settled in Britain. List out how you know what you know. Where does your knowledge and information come from? How much of it is based on first-hand experience? What do you think about this?

Finally, what do you think about the theory of Orientalism?

If possible, discuss your reflections in a small group.

Open and closed views of the 'other'

At the turn of the millennium (2000), the Runnymede Trust, an independent think-tank, produced the last of a series of reports entitled *The Future of Multi-Ethnic Britain – The Parekh Report*, which was launched by the then Secretary of State Jack Straw. The report was the work of Bikhu Parekh and is an interesting and extensive analysis of multi-cultural Britain. However, for the purpose of this chapter, the focus is a model, adapted and developed from an earlier Runnymede Trust Report *Islamaphobia: A Challenge for Us All* (1997) by Parekh. The model, located in the heart of the 417 pages, helps identify perceptions and attitudes to differences, in the form of 'the other', by distinguishing between two categories of 'closed' and 'open' views of the 'other'. The model takes the reader through eight 'distinctions' (see the model below, Table 3.1), listing the 'closed' and 'open' views of 'the other'. I believe that in relation to professional practice, in all social care arenas (including youth and community work), this model provides an important 'check-up', food for questioning, self-reflection and potential development and even change for practitioners and for the individuals, groups and communities with whom they work. The model provides a way of honestly appraising one's own views and perceptions of people that are different from oneself, i.e. of 'the other', and through the 'open views of the other' category, it provides the necessary goal to strive for in relation to one's attitudes and perceptions to differences.

With its categorisation of 'closed' and 'open' views of 'the other', for me this model synthesises much of the preceding discussion in relation to oppression, the principles of equity and equality and Said's (1978) theory of Orientalism. It is therefore important to spend some time thinking about each of the distinctions on the model below (Table 3.1).

ACTIVITY 3.7

This exercise is best undertaken individually to help with self-reflection. Select a group or community that is different from your own (this can be in terms of religion, culture or race). Then take each of the distinctions covered by Parekh's (2000) model and try, as honestly as possibly, to identify the extent to which you have 'closed' or 'open' views of 'the other' group or community you have selected.

For each of the distinctions, examine where your 'closed' and/or 'open' views may have come from.

Table 3.1 Closed and Open Views of the Other.

Distinctions	Closed views of the other	Open views of the other
1 Monolithic/diverse	The other seen as a single monolithic bloc, static and unresponsive to new realities	The other seen as diverse and progressive, with internal differences, debates and development
2 Separate/interacting	The other seen as separate: (a) not having any aims or values in common with the self; (b) not affected by it; (c) not influencing it	The other seen as independent with the self: (a) having certain values and aims; (b) affected by it; (c) enriching it
3 Inferior/different	The other seen as inferior to the self: e.g. barbaric, irrational, 'fundamentalist'	The other seen as different but of equal worth
4 Enemy/partner	The other seen as violent, aggressive, threatening, to be defeated and perhaps dominated	The other seen as an actual or potential partner in joint co-operative enterprises and in the solution of shared problems
5 Manipulative/sincere	The other seen as manipulative and deceitful, bent only on material or strategic advantage	The other seen as sincere in their beliefs, not hypocritical
6 Criticisms of the self rejected/considered	Criticisms made by the other of the self are rejected out of hand	Criticisms of the self are considered and debated
7 Discrimination defended/ not defended	Hostility towards the other used to justify discriminatory practices and exclusions of the other from mainstream society	Debates and disagreements with the other do not diminish efforts to combat discrimination and exclusion
8 Hostility towards the other seen as natural/ problematic	Fear and hostility towards the other accepted as natural and 'normal'	Critical views of the other themselves subjected to critique, lest they be inaccurate and unfair

Source: Parekh (2000, page 247).

Hegemony

The final section of this chapter will focus on the theory of hegemony. As a youth and community practitioner, I have found this theory fundamental in shedding light on the existing and continuing inequalities in any society. It has helped me understand the negotiation of power relations in society, which help to maintain the status quo, while also suggesting ways in which this could be challenged, especially by professionals such as youth and community workers who are well placed to be catalysts for change in society.

The theory is the work of Antonio Gramsci, who was born in 1891 and died in prison in 1937. He was an Italian Marxist, founder of the Italian Communist Party, an intellectual, journalist and was considered a major theoretician who languished for the last 11 years of his life in Mussolini's prisons. During his time in prison, Gramsci wrote and smuggled out 32 notebooks, which were translated into English in the 1970s. As a Marxist, the central question and fundamental to his theory of hegemony was the concern with the failure of Marxist analyses of society to explain why change does not take place and more specifically why there is a failure for revolutions to occur to change the nature of an oppressive, bourgeoisie-controlled state. In short, Marxist analysis was inadequate to explain an on-going status quo.

The word 'hegemony' comes from Greek philosophy, 'hegemonia' to mean 'authority'. The dictionary definition of 'hegemony' (Collins, 1998, page 716) is 'ascendancy or domination of one power or state within a league, confederation, etc., or of one social class over others'. The concern, therefore, with control, authority and power in society is clear. The theory of hegemony helps explain how control is maintained by particular groups in society.

Through his detailed reflections (captured in his notebooks), Gramsci suggested that ideology plays a key role in the maintenance of this control and authority. Giddens (1997, page 583) defines ideology as 'shared ideas or beliefs which serve to justify the interests of dominant groups'. It therefore has a close relationship with power, helping to legitimise the differential power that different groups and communities hold in a society, which in turn can influence the perceptions that people hold in the society in which they live. In short, as Burke (1999, and 2005, page 2) suggests: '… it distorts the real situation that people find themselves in'.

Popple (2000, page 45) makes the significance of ideas and ideology to the theory of hegemony very clear:

> *To achieve an effective hegemony, Gramsci argued, there must be a number of beliefs or ideas which are generally accepted by all but which serve to justify the interests of the dominant groups. These images, concepts and ideas 'make sense' of everyday experiences are collectively known as 'ideology'. Gramsci argues that ideology is the cement that keeps society together.*

Gramsci realised that economic control and the political force of the ruling classes may be necessary, as propounded by traditional Marxist theory, but insufficient to perpetuate its rule. Such 'naked' oppression could inspire revolution. What is necessary to perpetuate control for the ruling classes is to secure the consent of the subordinate classes and the method of control is not naked force, but ideology, philosophy and intellectualism. How this is achieved, according to Connell (1995, page 77), is through a 'cultural dynamic'.

> *The concept of 'hegemony', deriving from Antonio Gramsci's analysis of class relations, refers to the cultural dynamic by which a group claims and sustains a leading position in social life.*

As discussed in an earlier chapter, culture is difficult to define and permeates numerous aspects of our lives. It would perhaps be easier to understand the theory by applying it to a specific example. One such simple example could be the notion of the 'nuclear' family. We all belong to families and know that families take many forms, yet the notion of the ideal, nuclear family perpetuates, in spite of the growing significance of one-parent families and changes taking place especially in Western cultures (because of the fast changing economic role of women in societies) (González-López, 2002). Why does the 'ideal' image persist? What part, for instance, do the media and the institutions of religion and education play in this? This example illustrates the deep-seated hegemonic control that can exist in relation to perception, reality and our acceptance of things 'as they are'.

The propensity to 'go along' with the status quo in spite of our real experiences suggesting a different story concerns the process of acquiescence. The prevailing ideas in society are promoted by those in power as normal and natural, and accepted uncritically and unconsciously or, as Slattery (2003, page 225) suggests '... at least [by] acquiescence'.

Gramsci's (1971) theory of hegemony is described by Burke (1999 and 2005, page 3) as 'a far more subtle theory of power than any of his contemporaries' which requires an ideological bond between the rulers and the ruled'.

To challenge hegemonic processes in society, Gramsci (1971) advocated the creation of counter hegemony. Since ideology is central for hegemony, it is not surprising that Gramsci considered the role of intellectuals being important in both hegemony and counter hegemony. His definition of an intellectual, however, is not limited to the classical notion of an academic or philosopher. Burke (1999 and 2005, page 4) explains:

> *Gramsci's notebooks are quite clear on the matter. He writes that 'all men are intellectual [and presumably women] but not all men have in society the function of intellectuals'. What he meant by that was that everyone has an intellect and uses it but not all are intellectuals* **by social function***.*

To change the status quo through the development of a counter hegemony which would challenge the 'common sense' view of society, it was necessary for well-placed individuals and groups in society to develop an alternative philosophy, ideology and intellectualism, and be the intellectuals in the counter hegemonic process. It was also important to widen the circle of those involved in the counter hegemony by building more and more alliances with like-minded people and, importantly, become involved in empowering 'the populace' to believe in themselves and the 'cause' and through this new knowledge and education, encourage active participation and action to bring about change.

It is not difficult to see why youth and community workers are potentially so well placed to challenge hegemonic processes in society. They have a real potential to be the well-placed 'intellectuals' in a counter hegemony. Popple discusses the role of community workers in regard to this:

In this paradigm community workers are situated in a pivotal position within the civil society, for although they are employees of the state and are required to play a part in maintaining the social system, they are not necessarily in agreement with its ideology. Accordingly, community workers have opportunities to work alongside members of communities as they articulate their contradictory understanding of the world and their situation within it.

(2000, page 46)

The theory of hegemony is an important aid for understanding the political and socio-economic positions of relative groups in society. More specifically, the theory highlights the role played by ideology in the control over society maintained by those in power. The use of counter hegemony, and therefore the ability to think differently, empowers others through an educative process of active participation, and the importance of self-reflection and reflective practice is enshrined in youth and community work, making such practitioners well placed to encourage the necessary challenges to bring about change. In doing so, youth and community practitioners need to recognise and understand the hegemonic processes operating in society.

ACTIVITY 3.8

Consider (individually or in a small group) each of the four scenarios below. In relation to each, consider the role potentially played by hegemony and think about how and why hegemonic processes are evident.

SCENARIO 1

Having completed an input to staff at a local school on the detached project which employs him, Paul arrives for his detached work session (on the streets) still dressed in a shirt, tie and jacket. His team member offers him a sweatshirt before they go out onto the streets.

> SCENARIO *2*
>
> *You've managed to get hold of a few free tickets to a local football derby (the Blues vs the Reds). The four young people you take to the match are all 'Blues' supporters. However, when you get to the match you find that the seats are all in with the 'Reds' supporters.*

> SCENARIO *3*
>
> *After the youth club session is over, Claire, one of the sessional workers, goes to the 'Ladies' and gets changed into her going out clothes, because she is meeting some friends in town to go on to a birthday party in a night club. A male member of staff whistles and comments on how 'sexy' she looks as she comes out.*

> SCENARIO *4*
>
> *A female Asian youth worker goes to the local secondary school in a predominantly Asian area of the city to recruit members to a local girls' cub. She is dressed in a T-shirt and a skirt just above the knees. The community liaison worker at the school, an older Asian man, calls her into his office and asks, "Why should we allow you to recruit these girls when you are clearly setting a bad example?"*

C H A P T E R   R E V I E W

This chapter explored some of the concepts and theories significant for understanding work with diversity. In doing so, it also examined the impact and interplay between power and authority in relation to the different cultural communities in any multi-cultural society. In particular, it discussed the concepts of oppression, equity and equality, and the theories of Orientalism (Said, 1978) and hegemony (Gramsci, 1971). It also explored Parekh's (2000) 'open' and 'closed' categories for perceiving, stereo-typing and interacting with 'the other', in relation to difference.

FURTHER READING

Burke, B (1999, 2005) Antonio Gramsci, and Education, *the encyclopedia of informal education*, www.infed.org/thinkers/et-gram.htm

Burke provides a good overview to the life, work and ideas of Gramsci, and therefore the theory of hegemony.

Parekh, B (2000) *The Future of Multi-Ethnic Britain: The Parekh Report*. London: Profile Books.

This is a comprehensive report that maps the state of multi-cultural Britain and includes the model included in this chapter on open and closed views of the other.

Chapter 4
Trust and 'storying' in practice

Achieving your Youth and Community Work degree

The Professional and National Occupational Standards for youth work covered by this chapter are:

1.3.1   Facilitate young people's exploration of their value and beliefs

2.3.2   Develop a culture and systems that promote equality and value diversity

3.1.2   Assist young people to express and realise their goals

3.3.1   Develop productive working relationships with colleagues

3.3.2   Develop productive working relationships with colleagues and stakeholders

5.1.1   Work as an effective and reflective practitioner

Introduction

This chapter begins with a focus on the notion of 'trust' and moves onto the significance of stories (one's own and those of others) for youth and community work practice. The relationship between the concept of trust and being able to both trust others and create a trusting environment in which they can tell their stories and enable you to tell yours is not always an obvious one, especially in the context of working with diversity. However, in relation to working with people who are different from oneself as a practitioner, the notion of trust is, perhaps, even more significant than in 'normal' practice, where it is clearly accepted as an important aspect of youth and community work.

Fear of the 'other', ignorance and stereotyping often lead us to make judgments and assumptions about others who are different from us (Parekh, 2000). It is through the nurturing of trusting relationships that we begin to understand and learn about others because trusting relationships are an inevitable consequence of meaningful experience of the other and therefore fundamental for dispelling our fears and pre-conceived notions and judgements of those that are different from us. When practitioners manage to create the optimum environment for a relationship with a young person, member of the community and/or a colleague who is different from themselves, then trust underpins the relationship, and the 'telling' of each other's stories becomes possible.

Trust and working with diversity

The National Youth Agency's Statement of Values and Principles on *Ethical Conduct in Youth Work* is clear that trust between workers and young people and trust between organisations and services and parents and young people are fundamental underpinning elements of the behaviour of everyone involved in youth work and youth services (NYA cited in Harrison and Wise, 2005, page 18). Therefore, in relation to ethical practice the significance of trust is given.

In their exploration of conversation as the 'stock and trade' of youth and community practice, Jeffs and Smith remind us that:

> Unlike school teachers we have no national curriculum to fall back on, no examinations holding a promise of employment. We have nothing to sustain a learning relationship after indifference, even loathing has supplanted respect. Thus, moral authority – being seen by others as people with integrity, wisdom and an understanding of right and wrong – is something we must seek and preserve.

(2005, page 99)

Conversation clearly involves effective interpersonal skills and effective communication. This along with the importance of trust as a factor is acknowledged by the Department for Educations and Skills (DfES), which states that:

> A key part of effective communication and engagement is trust, both between the workforce, children, young people and their carers, and between and within different sectors of the workforce itself.

(DfES, 2003, page 6)

Furthermore, it states that in relation to the 'skills' required for safeguarding and promoting the welfare of the child, it is important to establish rapport and respectful, trusting relationships with children, young people and those caring for them (DFES, 2003, page 13).

The basis of work with young people and within communities in general is therefore heavily reliant on how adept we are at developing conversations and establishing rapport. As Jeffs and Smith (2005, pages 39–40) in their chapter on 'Trusting in Conversation' simply point out:

> *Conversation is both the medium through which we work and it involves many of the qualities we seek to foster as educators:*
>
> - *concern for others*
> - *trust*
> - *respect for others – and ourselves*
> - *affection*

All of the above can take time and be achieved through the process of developing a relationship, but perhaps, in the context of working with diversity, the idea of developing respect for others in relation to ourselves is particularly significant and trust is the critical ingredient for this to succeed. Once this is addressed, the other elements outlined above may naturally follow. It is therefore not surprising, for example, that in relation to mentoring relationships between young people and adults Styles and Morrow (1995) found that unless a trusting relationship was in place between mentors and their young mentees, the mentoring arrangement and relationship was much more likely to fail or be terminated.

The idea that youth workers, just like mentors (in a more formalised sense), can act as role models is not exactly new and neither is the sense that being a role model involves, among other things, 'building relationships that are open, honest and based on trust' (Ingram and Harris, 2005, page 15), both with young people as practitioners and in enabling them in turn to do so with those around them. Indeed, Jeffs and Smith (2005) suggest that practitioners face inevitable scrutiny from those they work with and alongside: 'There will be those seeking a role model and others straining to detect hypocrisy' (page 97).

In relationships and conversations between people who are very different from each other and come from different cultural contexts, avoiding the whiff of 'hypocrisy' along with the fear of saying 'the wrong thing' or 'offending' can be daunting and can easily generate mistrust. The art of conversation is in itself a complicated and sophisticated activity. As Wardhaugh (1985, page 4) points out:

> *You must have a well-developed feeling about what you can (or cannot) say and when you can (or cannot) speak. You must know how to use words to do things and also exactly what words you can use in certain circumstances. And you must be able to supplement and reinforce what you choose to say with other appropriate behaviours: your movements, gestures posture, gaze, and so on. You must also attune yourself to how others employ these same skills.*

CASE STUDY: TOO SPICY

Sarah works in a multi-cultural area in a team which includes a colleague from Sri Lanka called Lakshmi. Sarah was appointed to her post at the same time as her Sri Lankan colleague became a member of the team. As a result, having started at the same time, they both feel that they have something in common.

However, Sarah is becoming more and more conscious that she keeps making excuses every time Lakshmi asks her to come round for something to eat. Sarah assumes that a meal at Lakshmi's would be too spicy and she really hates spicy food and curry. She doesn't want to say that to Lakshmi because she doesn't want to offend her.

ACTIVITY **4.1**

Think about the situation above and consider why Sarah is feeling the way she is. What is the result of her actions on her relationship with Lakshmi and why? How much trust is evident in this relationship and does it matter?

Clearly, in situations where there is a lack of understanding, knowledge and experience, or indeed, any knowledge or understanding may be based on stereotypical perceptions, then the basis for 'attuning' oneself to the 'other' person is fraught with uncertainties. The important element of trust is inevitably far removed in such a situation. Jeffs and Smith suggest that people in such cases can feel clumsy, or have difficulties in this area. They strike a simple note of caution: 'This means that conversations between people of different cultures require special care' (2005, page 30).

I believe that conversations and relationships between people who are culturally very different from each other need special care, more than most, and also need to be built on the following:

Realness in the facilitator of learning (i.e. genuineness or congruence).

Prizing, acceptance, trust (i.e. unconditional positive regard).

Empathic Understanding (i.e. empathy).

(Rogers, 1983, pages 121–126)

However, therein lies the complexity or difficulty that surely such core conditions prized in youth and community work as in other social care fields are inevitably more difficult to establish and maintain in circumstances where the spectre of 'difference' looms between people. It becomes even more fraught and, perhaps, even

43

impossible if there is a hint of closed views and perceptions of the other (Parekh, 2000), as discussed in Chapter 3.

To be effective, it is very important for the youth and community workers to be aware of the fact that each person with whom they work has 'a unique set of perceptions and experiences' (Crosby, 2005, page 96). However, often pressures within work can make this difficult to comprehend, because such awareness needs and takes time and often the understanding only emerges as a relationship gradually develops. Significantly, the knowledge, appreciation and understanding we develop of others is inevitably filtered through the ways in which we have made sense of our own experiences. In fact, the basis of empathy lies in this fact. Crosby also states:

> Of course, we can never view other people in ways which are value free, objective or neutral because our perceptions will always be filtered through the many layers of our own experience. So a vital part of informal educators' 'internal work' is in seeking to recognise and reduce the effects of distortions in their perceptions of the other person. This entails submitting their perceptions to a continuous process of reflection, checking and analysis.

> (2005, page 98)

When we work to really understand others in a deep sense, it inevitably means, as Peck (1990) suggests, 'extending ourselves'. The process has to, by its very nature, mean that we push the boundaries of our own understanding, feelings and knowledge, and this then leads to challenging our perceptions and assumptions and any existing prejudices. The process of extending ourselves, when it concerns two or more individuals within it, needs to be taking place in all those involved and it is inevitable that where this is truly present it can lead to change. Rogers (1961, page 33), when reflecting on the role of a facilitator, points out:

> If I can provide a certain type of relationship, the other person will discover within (themselves) the capacity to use that relationship for growth, and change and personal development will occur.

In situations where difference is a significant element of the relationship between people, this process can be difficult and daunting and, in fact, anything that leads to a change in us is feared. Where trust is a significant basis of a relationship, then perhaps it becomes easier to engage with such a process, because the existence of trust facilitates Rogers' (1983) congruence and empathy and enables us to be open and ask what we need to ask to deepen our understanding, especially, of those who are different from us. It, in fact, facilitates the shift in our perceptions and attitudes from what Parekh (2000) describes as closed views to more open views of the other. This discussion reminds me of a heated exchange that took place between an African-Caribbean colleague and me some years ago. We were working on an inter-faith/religious/cultural weekend residential, where she was a volunteer and I had taken along a group of young Asian women. Other workers had come along with young women from different cultural, religious and ethnic backgrounds. The focus of the weekend was to celebrate difference and affirm inter-cultural links.

The young Asian women in my group were all bi-lingual, but I knew from my prior relationship with them that they felt self-conscious about admitting to this and using their Punjabi-speaking skills. They seemed almost embarrassed about admitting to being able to speak Punjabi. On the first day of the residential, at lunchtime, my African-Caribbean colleague came and joined my group at our table. At some point during lunch, I asked one of the young women to pass the salt and pepper in Punjabi, a language that I had in common with the young women in my group and I consciously used it with them whenever possible, because I thought this would help them to be less self-conscious about using it. I have never forgotten the reaction from my African-Caribbean colleague. She said angrily, 'Have some manners; don't be so rude; you should speak in English'. The episode escalated and led to fiery debate and lots of soul searching but, ultimately, what I realised was that there was clearly little or no trust in the relationship that we had with each other. It was simply all to do with trust or the lack of it. I had, unknowingly and without thinking, used my first language to communicate about something mundane to the young women in my group, but my colleague perhaps had assumed that I was making a comment on her behind her back and therefore at the very least I was being rude and at worst, utterly unprofessional. Recovering from such a position in a public forum was difficult for both of us. However, I really learnt a lot from the incident and hope that it proved just as educational for her.

The following activity illustrates some of the dilemmas faced in situations where difference and the inter-play between being an insider or an outsider to a group can pose challenges to the decisions faced by practitioners.

CASE STUDY: CHALLENGING BEHAVIOUR

Naz works as a detached worker with two other colleagues. She is Bangladeshi by origin and her colleagues are both White Europeans, who have lived all their lives in the UK.

The workers are travelling in a mini-bus to the local cinema for an outing, along with nine young people. Six of these nine young people are Bangladeshis and the rest are White Europeans. There is a lot of banter in the mini-bus. However, at one point, a couple of the Bangladeshis say something in Bengali that makes the other Bangladeshis roar with laughter. Naz understood the sexist comments that have been made in Bengali and knows that she needs to challenge the behaviour.

However, how should she do this? In which language (Bengali or English) should she challenge the young people and why?

ACTIVITY **4.2**

You can reflect on this exercise on your own or discuss it in a small group.

What do you think Naz should have done, and consider the consequences of whichever action she chose to take regarding:

a) her relationship with her colleagues;

b) her relationship with the White European young people;

c) her relationship with the Bangladeshi young people.

What are the consequences of the decision she made, and why does it even matter?

So far, the significance of trust for conversation and for relationships between people, especially those where cultural difference (in its broadest sense) is a factor, has been discussed. However, the link between trust and the other key focus of this chapter, stories and 'storying' needs further reflection. Collander-Brown (2005) coins the term 'working alliance' (page 33) to describe the necessity of openness, trust and honesty in the relationship that youth and community workers develop with those individuals with whom they work. The existence of such a relationship is necessary if it is to facilitate, especially in his case, young people telling their stories to the practitioners who work with them. As he eloquently states:

> *In building a working alliance, workers begin to understand the story of the other. As a child, when read or told a story I remember the blank anticipation. I had no idea what was coming and my mind was free and waiting. It was as if I made or found the space in my mind for what was to come. This image, of* **making a space in the mind***, illustrates what happens next in the process of* **being with another** *as a professional practitioner... Each person has their own unique story comprising both life events... and the way the individual experiences and attempts to make sense of these events over the life course. Being* **with** *someone involves gradually gathering up aspects of this combination of events and understandings so the sense of their uniqueness begins to unfold. No-one ever fully understands what it is like to be another person.*

(Collander-Brown, 2005, page 33)

Although Collander-Brown is clearly right in suggesting that 'no-one ever fully understands what it is like to be another person', perhaps, listening to someone's story is the closest you can get to having some understanding and therefore developing an empathy for who they are and what they have experienced.

Facilitating the telling of one's story clearly needs the 'right' ambience, environment and relationship to be established. This is only possible if the storyteller feels actively listened to. As Bowler (2010, page 44) points out:

The way we listen to others, and hear and interpret others' stories is intricately interwoven with the way we tell our stories and how we explain the central aspects of our own development.

Therefore, personal stories provide a way of comparing and contrasting our lives to those of others, which can help us better understand both those we listen to and ourselves. In short, they enable us to 'make sense' of our life, construct a narrative around it and therefore reflect on what has shaped our life. In the words of Lawler (2002, page 250):

...narrative... both connotes and constitutes movement – the movement from the potential to the actual, from what could be to what is, from past to present, from present to future.

Roberts (1994, page 13) makes a slightly different but significant point, when she suggests that our stories often 'resonate' with those of others and thus contribute to the ability to empathise. An example from my own life is the story of migration, which has been a recurring theme in my life and the life of my family. My maternal grandfather migrated from Punjab in India to Kenya, to work on the railways for the British who were the colonial rulers in both India and Kenya at the time. Later, my father also migrated from India to Kenya to marry my mother, and then, when I was nine years old, my parents and I with my siblings migrated to England. This aspect of my life resonates both with my parents' and grandparent's stories, and with the stories of others who have migrated and settled in Britain. The notion of resonance has a way, therefore, of binding your story to those of others. Roberts (1994, page 5) simply suggests that hearing one story usually triggers another story. She also emphasises the fact that each of us likes to be noticed, to feel unique:

We all need to be seen and heard, to be known for our unique life experiences. We all carry our stories with us and when we tell them to others they have the power to link us together.

(Roberts, 1994, page xiv)

When you consider your own story, or even tell your story using the timeline suggested in Chapter 1, you may find, as Shank (1990, page 12) states, 'human memory is story-based'. Stories, which answer key questions such as when? where? how? what? with whom? etc., provide us with a way of indexing or organising our thoughts and experiences in a coherent way (Shank, 1990). The organising of the different elements that make up one's story is usually guided by what Giddens (1991, page 113) describes as 'fateful moments' and Denzin (1989, page 33) calls 'epiphanies'.

This interplay, the telling of and listening to stories, is important in enabling us to gage what is considered 'normal' within a society and by inference; we can perhaps recognise that which may fall outside the boundaries of 'normality'. The wider socio-political context in which stories give shape to the life of the 'teller' is often very significant. For example, clearly the brutality of Hitler's regime would have an indelible effect on the life of any Jewish person who experienced it and lived to tell the story. Therefore, as Bowler (2010, page 45) states:

> *It is important to recognise that our experiences, the ways we express them and the meanings we derive from them are not an objective account of facts. They happen in a political context where social and cultural practices are produced and reproduced. While exploring individual life stories we also need to consider the 'social world' people inhabit and distinguish between what could be termed biographical 'facts' and which elements are socially constructed.*

In fact, the telling of our stories enables us to make difficult connections between our private and public worlds. Yolen (1986, page 13) describes the process aptly when she says, 'Storytelling is a personal art that makes public what is private and makes private what is public'.

This link between the private and the public is an important vehicle for communicating experiences, especially, for those people who feel marginalised or are the minority within a particular society. This includes those who are alienated socially and in other ways, but may also include others who are merely different from the majority. Therefore, in a society which includes ethnic, racial, religious and other forms of diversity, storying can be a good way to forge understanding between people who are different from each other. However again, this is only possible if the listener can convey the fact that they care and want to listen. Roberts further points out: 'The same story is never told twice; depending on the audience, the place, the responses of the listeners and the questions, it will be modified and retold differently' (1994, page 10).

The telling of life stories by individuals has the power to move from the present to the family and community at large, and in doing so can, as Bowler (2010) suggested earlier, capture the social, political and historical context of the time. Thus my story of migration, mentioned briefly earlier, has the fervour of 'Africanisation' in Kenya, the political turmoil in Britain with Enoch Powell's 'Rivers of Blood' (1968) speech and anti-immigration assertions, and Idi Amin's madness and brutality in neighbouring Uganda all tied in with the story. The story of my family's migration from Kenya to Britain is therefore steeped in the socio-political contexts of the time, which have helped to give the story its uniqueness and significance in my life. This socio-political context for this part of my story has inevitably helped to shape who I am.

However, society has a way of placing limits on the stories that we are able to tell, and therefore on those that are heard. Bowler states: '… and thus, the telling of the story is embedded in the traditions of what social norms allow participants to share' (2010, page 48).

In every society, usually those who are the majority, or those who hold the power, merely because they are in the majority, are able to determine the 'social norms'. This power is subtle and can be transformed into the 'cultural imperialism' (Young, 1990) discussed in the previous chapter. Bowler explains the process thus:

> *The majority group is often everywhere and nowhere in public commentary. It is not uncommon that marginalized and less powerful groups find it difficult to feel represented or at home in the different public language that is available.*

> (2010, page 53)

This process in itself then contributes to the establishment of what I would describe as 'hierarchies' of stories in a society, making a direct link between the telling of stories and power in a society. In short, those who are able to tell their stories in a society have the power to contribute to the establishment of social norms, and therefore have the power to determine which individual or group can tell their story and which will be heard. It is not difficult, therefore, to make the link between this process and the theory of hegemony (Gramsci, 1971) discussed in the previous chapter. Those who can tell their stories in a society are likely to have a hegemonic control within that society.

Just as in the process of acquiring hegemonic influence or control in a society, the formal institutions within that society (such as those based around formal education and religion) play a part, so as Bowler points out, '…media acquire a normative function for governing private lives to a greater extent and therefore an important role in perpetuating dominant ideas' (2010, page 59).

This means that the stories of some sections, groups or communities in a society become subjugated or silenced. An example is highlighted by the family therapist Laird (1993) who suggests that women's stories in particular may be silenced in male-dominated paternalistic societies, or where men may largely have control of communication networks and the media. Therefore, women's stories of abuse, incest, harassment and violence may be regarded as 'taboo', which in turn helps to silence them. However, as Roberts states: 'There are important distinctions that need to be made between silence that invites talk and silence that pushes stories underground' (1994, page 9).

Silence that is chosen and used effectively as a means of communication can be a useful tool, but this is very different from the silence that may be inflicted on an individual, group or community as a result of powerlessness (Young, 1990) or not having a voice. As Bowler (2010, page 59) explains:

> *A further layer of subjugated knowledge arises from the possibility that some stories are not told at all. Some dominant societal concepts and norms can acquire a near mythical status and their validity is not questioned in a public domain. People whose actual experiences do not conform to these norms are therefore more likely to regard themselves as deficient rather than criticise the inappropriate norm.*

Therefore, not only there is a danger that an individual, group or community feels subjugated and silenced but also there is a danger that the individual group or community becomes at best stereotyped, and at worst, 'pathologised', being ascribed with traits that are considered abnormal. Clearly, when dealing with the notion of closed views of the other (Parekh, 2000) as discussed in the previous chapter, where the potential misunderstandings, distrust and even fear lurk just beneath the surface, those that are different are perhaps more likely to be prone to this process.

ACTIVITY **4.3**

Think of those stories and the groups to which they belong that are pushed 'underground'.

List as many of these as you can, using two columns, one for the topic or story and the other for the group to which it belongs. Then reflect on why these stories are considered to be underground and think about the relative position and power that the listed groups or communities have in British society today.

If possible, discuss your list in a small group.

Finally, Roberts provides a very useful way of categorising the different stories that exist in any society. Based on her work, as a family therapist, she describes these as 'story styles', as she explains:

> Sometimes family members come in with very **intertwined** stories, so that events that occurred at one time are used to interpret other circumstances. Other families present with very isolated or **separated** stories, where they don't see the connections between parallel incidents. Story resources may not be readily available to families in one or more parts of their lives because they have been **minimised** or **interrupted**. Or the stories may have been **silenced** or kept hidden or secret. **Rigid** stories are told the same way over and over and may lead to a set meaning of key events. In other parts of people's lives, stories may have **evolved** and developed flexibly over time, giving them access to different ways to examine their experiences.

(Roberts, 1994, page 12)

Although she does not suggest that her 'story styles' can be used to categorise stories that affect groups and communities (because her focus as a family therapist is only on the individual and their family), in fact, her categorisations are, I think, a very useful way of examining stories that link individuals to families, and then to the wider groups and communities to which they belong, in the context of the wider society. The 'story styles' therefore lend themselves well to the shift from the personal to the wider context in which the individual exists. The following table, adapted from Roberts (1994, page 13), captures the 'story styles' more succinctly.

STORY STYLES

INTERTWINED

- *One story resonates with another; time is not bound.*
- *Focus is on the parallels between situations/lives/life events or on making/ defining the story as the opposite of a previous story*
- *Meaning is passed on unchanged from the first story in time to the second*

DISTINCT/SEPARATED

- *Similar dilemmas, issues no linked*
- *Focus is on each individual story*
- *No access to meaning-making across different contexts*

MINIMAL/INTERRUPTED

- *Little access to historical time*
- *Few details to flesh out the stories*
- *Hard to make meaning from multiple perspectives*

SILENCED/SECRET

- *Hidden or subterranean text*
- *Story cannot be told*
- *Meaning is unclear, confusing; may contain hidden alliances or coalitions*

RIGID

- *Time is 'frozen'*
- *Text is unknown – others can tell the story*
- *Set interpretation of the meaning*

EVOLVING

- *Recognition that the story is different at different times of life*
- *The details and points that are emphasized change*
- *Places provided to keep making new message*

ACTIVITY **4.4**

a) *Consider each of the 'story styles' listed by Roberts (1994) and think of stories from your own life for each of the categories. If you are able to, then discuss each of the categories and the stories related to each of them with another person and encourage the other person to do the same.*

b) *Again, consider each of the 'story styles' listed by Roberts and think of stories told to you by the people you work with for each of the categories.*

ACTIVITY **4.4** *continued*

> *Alternatively, you may want to use the table as a tool and encourage those that you work with individually to share their stories in relation to Roberts' (1994) story styles.*
>
> *Please note that you may find that one story, in fact, can be included in more than one category.*

The first part of the previous exercise is a very good way of aiding reflection on your own life and may help you decide which stories you are able and willing to share with others. The second part of the exercise may help you to gain a deeper understanding of the lives of those whose stories you have listened.

CHAPTER REVIEW

This chapter explored the importance of trust as an integral aspect of youth and community practice, and suggested that its significance was heightened in relation to working with diversity. The exercises illustrate the potential dilemmas faced by practitioners in situations when working with diversity where trust-related considerations play a significant part. The telling of and listening to stories are then explored both as a 'natural' progression for professional relationships that are based on trust and as a tool for understanding relative power in relation to stories that can be told and those that are subjugated or silenced in society. The exercises related to 'storying' are meant to be a tool for self reflection and also a way of developing an understanding of the interplay between stories and power and the connections between personal stories and stories in a wider, societal context.

FURTHER READING

Bowler, R (2010) 'Learning from Lives, in Buchroth, I and Parkin, C (eds) *Using Theory in Youth and Community Practice*. Exeter: Learning Matters.

This is an interesting chapter that focuses on the importance of life experiences and the development of identity in work with young people and adults.

Jeffs, T and Smith, MK (2005) *Informal Education: Conversation, Democracy and Learning*, 3rd edition. Nottingham: Educational Heretics Press.

This is a key text that explores the 'everyday' tools of informal education such as the use of conversation.

Roberts, J (1994) *Tales and Transformations: Stories in Families and Family Therapy*. London: W. W. Norton and Company.

In this text Roberts explores the significance of stories in family contexts.

Chapter 5
Understanding the consequences of Islamophobia

Achieving your Youth and Community Work degree

The Professional and National Occupational Standards for youth work covered by this chapter are:

2.1.1	Ensure that the rights of young people are promoted and upheld
2.3.1	Promote equality of opportunity and diversity in your area of responsibility
2.3.2	Develop a culture and systems that promote equality and value diversity
2.3.3	Challenge oppressive behaviour in young people
4.1.1	Investigate the needs of young people and the community, in relation to youth work
5.1.1	work as an effective and reflective practitioner

Introduction

When I was thinking about what shape or form this chapter should take, there was a tangible sense of anxiety that I experienced. This was not just the result of the normal sense of apprehension a writer may feel when writing something for public and peer/editorial review – it was very different this time. I found myself making statements to a number of people (mostly friends) that with this chapter I had to be 'careful', this is a contentious subject.

On reflection, I think this anxiety came from my understanding that as an Asian in Britain, I was very much an 'insider' to this community. However, as a Hindu, I was an overt 'outsider' to the Muslim community in Britain and being identified as an outsider operated on many levels from the simplest, as someone merely belonging to a different religious community, to a position where some insiders to the Muslim community may perceive me as an interloper with no business being there given my identity as Hindu, based on the relationships between

Muslims and Hindus on the Indian sub-continent. On the other side, there were the 'other' communities in Britain, especially the white community, many of whom lack understanding and knowledge of the religious, ethnic and cultural diversity among Britain's Asian community, which would merely see me as an 'insider' and, therefore, even as a part of Britain's Muslim community. So, I had to tread carefully and this sense of angst perhaps captures the difficulty with the focus of the chapter.

As I was struggling with these dilemmas and thoughts, I recalled an incident with one of my students some years ago. She was a diligent student, a practicing Jew, who came for a tutorial. As we discussed the current assignment that she was seeking support with, she said:

> Sangeeta, I'm sorry I just need to apologise for something first. I
> know I really wasn't paying any attention last week in the lecture,
> but I just switched off as soon as you said you were going to discuss
> 'Islamophobia'. I just knew you would be sympathetic as a member of
> the community.

I recalled that I had started the lecture, in fact, by pointing out how much an outsider I was to the Muslim community and it was imperative that as an outsider, I understood and conveyed the significance for all of British society that it be understood and challenged. Her apology was a real disappointment, but it makes me even more determined to do justice to the subject.

Let's start by defining Islamophobia and then go on to explore its existence and rise in current British society. In doing so, it will draw on the theories and concepts discussed in previous chapters and demonstrate how, in fact, these apply to the particular case of Islamophobia.

In exploring the issue of Islamophobia in the context of British society, the discourse in this chapter will also highlight the challenges posed and the urgency of addressing Islamophobia, especially for social care professionals.

Defining Islamophobia

The Runnymede Trust, in its comprehensive report on the rise of Islamophobia during and following the Bosnian conflict and the first Gulf War, defines it as follows:

> The term Islamophobia refers to unfounded hostility towards Islam. It refers
> also to the practical consequences of such hostility in unfair discrimination
> against Muslim individuals and communities, and to the exclusion of Muslims
> from mainstream political and social affairs.

(Runnymede Trust, 1997, page 4)

The report was commissioned as a result of the acknowledged growth in prejudice, targeting Muslims in particular. As the authors of the report explain:

> *The word 'Islamophobia' has been coined because there is a new reality which needs naming: anti-Muslim. Prejudice has grown so considerably and so rapidly in recent years that a new item in the vocabulary is needed so that it can be identified and acted against*

> (Runnymede Trust, 1997, page 4).

Current trends in Islamophobia

The significance in the existence and rise of Islamophobia lies in the fact that it signals a move (in relation to prejudice) away from what people look like, which is purely racially motivated prejudice to what they believe. The focus becomes a religious entity, which ironically covers communities from many different racial backgrounds.

Sheridan (2006, page 317), for instance, based on her study investigating levels of self-reported racial and religious discrimination in a sample of 222 British Muslims, states that: 'Results suggest that religious affiliation may be a more meaningful predictor of prejudice than race or ethnicity'.

This point is also emphasised by Allen (2005, page 49):

> *While racism on the basis of markers of race obviously continues, a shift is apparent in which some of the more traditional and obvious markers have been displaced by newer and more prevalent ones of a cultural, socio-religious nature.*

Perhaps the two identities, inherent in early Islam, complicate the situation especially for those ignorant of the complexities. Simply, the first of these relates to identity in relation to a particular Islamic religious belief and the second to the identity of politics which Islamic societies engender. For followers of Islam, these two identities help to distinguish between true believers and political affirmation. However, these often merge and are indistinguishable for those outside, thus resulting possibly in miscomprehension and fear of the unknown.

For young Muslims living in Britain, the fact that their lives may often be interrupted in the light of external events, including those from national and international politics (such as the present concern with terrorism and Muslims/the Islamic world), results in a politics of identity from which perhaps there is little or no escape. As Parekh (2000) described, the fact that communities under attack often will 'close ranks' and 'turn inwards' means that for young Muslims in Britain the outward symbols of their identity, expressed especially through how they dress and who they hang out with, inevitably take on a greater significance. Khan (2006), in the introduction to a special edition of Youth and Policy (No. 92, Summer 2006) focusing on Muslim youth work, points out that:

For most young people religiosity is a choice activated by whatever circumstances are presented by life, or not as the case may be. This is no longer necessarily so for Muslim young people, here it is activated by an Islamophobic discourse that does not allow this to be either latent or private.

On an anecdotal level, I can recall many occasions on which my mother has returned from a shopping trip to the local high street, and exclaimed:

You know that young Pakistani girl who is always so polite and always speaks to me. Well, I nearly didn't recognise her today, she's started to cover her head. She had such beautiful hair.

The fact that more and more Muslims, especially Asian Muslims, are using dress codes such as the hijab (head scarf) to distinguish themselves from other Asians and be clearly identified as Muslims in British society is part of the expression of an identity forged in the present climate.

Allen and Neilson (2002) for example suggest that visual identity as a Muslim is the key factor in determining whether an individual or group is the target for an attack. They, in fact, suggested that Muslim women wearing the hijab (head scarf) were more likely to be victims than the men, because they were more easily identifiable as Muslims.

CASE STUDY: WEARING THE HIJAB

Jackie, an African-Caribbean female youth worker, working in a racially mixed community, decided to convert to Islam some years ago. Her colleagues, who she has worked with for a couple of years, are aware that she is a Muslim, but have never asked her about her religion. None of her three colleagues are Muslims, and not many of the Muslims within the wider community are aware that Jackie is a Muslim. She has never really felt the need to discuss it.

However, one day Jackie decided to start wearing the hijab (head scarf). As she walked into work as usual, she became very conscious that her colleagues were avoiding making eye contact with her. She was taken aback and felt hurt.

ACTIVITY 5.1

Consider the case study above and think about why Jackie may have decided to wear the hijab and about her colleagues' reaction to her. Why is the wearing of a head scarf of significance? What would you have done in a similar situation?

If possible, discuss your thoughts in a small group.

The link between prejudice, lack of experience, knowledge and understanding of those that are different from us and with stereotyping has been discussed in a previous chapter. However, it is important, in relation to exploring the existence and rise in Islamophobia, to discuss this here in the context of this chapter. In the absence of 'real-life' experience, the media plays a crucial role in influencing perceptions and also informing gaps in knowledge.

Saeed, in his article on the Media, Racism and Islamophobia, states:

> *It is suggested that the representation of British Muslims echoes previous research on how minority groups are portrayed in the media. In many respects, the media representation of minority groups is a 'double-edged sword'. First, it marginalizes minority voices, thus they are virtually ignored or invisible (Saeed, 1999). Simultaneously actual representation of minority groups is often construed in negative discourses (Hartmann and Husband, 1974). When these frameworks are applied to audiences who have little social contact with minority groups, the role of the media as sole provider (or primary definer (Hall, 1978)) becomes crucial. (Van Dijk, 1991)*

> (Saeed, 2007, page 444)

As suggested above, Hartmann and Husband (1974, page 44) in their book *Racism and the Mass Media*, concluded that often minorities were presented as a problem:

> *... the perspective that coloured people are presented as ordinary members of society has become increasingly overshadowed by a news perspective in which that are presented as a problem.*

Consequently it was recognised by researchers relatively early on that the media discourse on ethnic minorities presented them as problematic and therefore contributed to the process of their 'othering', thus their distancing from being legitimate members of British society. This process, as Saeed (2007, pages 451–452) suggests in his discussion on media representations of Islam and Muslims, has a history and is influenced by wider national and global events:

> *During the late 1980s and continuing into the 1990s, interest in the whole Muslim community in the UK increased significantly. Beginning with national issues such as the Rushdie affair and international matters such as the 1991 Gulf War, a series of events brought Muslims into the media spotlight and adversely affected the Muslim population in the UK. New components within racist terminology appeared, and were used in a manner that could be argued were deliberately provocative to bait and ridicule Muslims and other ethnic minorities.*

The link between national and international events and increasing media focus has already been made (Saeed, 2007). The focus on the East and, in this case, on Islam and Muslims has a legacy which has been framed by the theory of Orientalism

(Said, 1978), and which was discussed in an earlier chapter. The media representation of Islam and Muslims as Whittaker (2002, page 55) suggests is caricatured in the following way:

> *...four very persistent stereotypes that crop up time and time again in the different articles. These tells us Muslims are intolerant, misogynist, violent or cruel. And finally strange or different.*

The increased stereotypical media focus on the actual major events that have taken place featuring Muslims have worryingly resulted in greater attacks and open hostility towards Muslims in Britain and also in Europe (British Crime Survey 2000 – cited in Claney et al., 2001). Much of this abuse or victimisation is described as harassment, verbal abuse and aggression (Allen and Neilsen, 2002).

Sheridan's research cited earlier concluded the following:

> *What was clear from the current work was that the sample of 222 UK Muslims reported highly significant increases in both implicit and more overt negative experiences on the basis of their race and religion. The sample reported that they were regularly ignored, overlook, stared at, surveyed, insulted, treated with suspicion, and physically attacked. They also reported observing anti-Islamic prejudice and discrimination at community and at national and international levels. These experiences all increased significantly following Bar-Tal and Labin's (2001) conclusion that major political events can influence how other groups are viewed. The current work demonstrated that major events may also affect how minority groups are treated at an everyday level. The evidence suggests that religion, in this case Islam, may be a more important determinant of discussion than is race or ethnicity.*

> (2006, page 334)

Alongside the obvious influence of the media, which has been explored in some depth, Mukhopadhyay (2007, page 102) also suggests:

> *There is 'the emergence of an alarmist scholarship in mainstream societies in Europe', which depicts a Europe flooded by Muslims in the form of legal and illegal immigrants; larger metropoles under threat of attack from underground Islamic terrorists who are just 'in our midst' or 'within' multiculturalism under threat and tolerance of the host societies touching its limit*

Such scholarship echoed other work such as Huntington's (1996) *The Clash of Civilizations and the Remaking of World Order*, which claimed:

> *The underlying problem for the West is not Islamic fundamentalism, it is Islam, a different civilisation whose people are convinced of the superiority of their culture and are obsessed with the inferiority of their power.*

> (page 217)

Such scholarship just contributes to painting Islam and Muslims as a homogenous entity posing a threat to the non-Muslim world. In short, it re-enforces the 'battle lines' between them and us, rather than nurturing any cross-cultural, cross-religious understanding or, more importantly, dialogue.

ACTIVITY **5.2**

Consider the cartoon from The Sun newspaper (21–6–2006). It first appeared during the media discussion concerning a teaching assistant who said that she wanted to wear her nijab (full covering) in school when she was working there.

Reflect on both the subtlety and the audacity of the image drawn. Note how there is absolutely no reference to Islam or Muslims and yet the image clearly captures a stereotype and insinuates much more.

What insinuations are made by this cartoon?

"WHAT! YOU EXPECT ME TO TEACH THESE STUDENTS UNMASKED?"

Figure 5.1 Stereotypes and prejudices. Reprinted with permission from © NI Syndication, London (2006).

Apart from the tragedy of the obvious victimisation of communities on the grounds of their religious allegiance and practice, signified by the rise in Islamophobia, another unfortunate consequence has been the disintegration of a united Asian identity. The processes leading to the rise and maintenance of Islamophobia has led to divisions on the lines of us and them, further entrenching the othering processes. As Cottle (2000, page 2) states:

It is in and through representations, for example, that members of the media audience are variously invited to construct a sense of who 'we' are in relation to who 'we' are not, whether as 'us' and 'them', 'insider' and 'outsider'... the 'west' and the 'rest'.

In regard to this, on 5 September 2005, following the July 7 bombings in London, *The Guardian* reported the following: 'If you travel on London's public-transport system you may have spotted them: stickers and T-shirts with "Don't freak, I'm a Sikh" written across them'.

Later on in the same article, the author writing under a pseudonym includes the views of Roger Ballard, a well-known researcher on Asian communities settled in Britain.

According to Roger Ballard, director of the Centre for Applied South Asian Studies at Manchester University, this polarisation on religious grounds, particularly between Muslims and non-Muslims, is growing. He thinks that young Asians don't hang together as much as they used to, especially at university. 'They've been educated in barmy notions of political identity', he says. Where the immigrant generation saw a common tie to South Asia, these young Britons focus on religious differences, and often get their information from extremist sources. 'They have no access to their culture, so instead they embrace a very crude form of identity politics.'

In some cases, as Sheridan (2006, page 319) also suggests, this inclination of non-Muslim Asians to separate themselves from the Muslim communities of Britain have led to the development of some very unlikely alliances: 'For instance, in the United Kingdom, the ultra right-wing British National Party formed an anti-Muslim alliance with Sikh and Hindu extremists'.

The fact that prejudice and stereotyping aided by the media and some academic discourse result in the processes related to Islamophobia has been explored in some depth. In evidence and relevance to these processes are the theories of Orientalism, Othering (based on the binary system of open and closed views) and hegemony. Saeed points out:

Islamophobia, like the colonial discourse of its predecessor, Orientalism, does not allow for diversity; contradictions and semiotic tensions are ignored as the homogenising ethnocentric template of otherness assumes that there is only one interpretation of Islam.

(2007, page 457)

The media's influence in shaping the perceptions of the public about Muslims and Islam shows how the media acts as an elite force controlling what and how we should think, in line with Gramsci's (1971) theory of hegemony. As Hall (1978, page 95) suggests, the media is responsible for developing and maintaining a 'machinery of representation', responsible for,

> ...*what and who gets represented and what and who routinely gets left out (and) how things, people, events, relationships get represented... the structure of access to the media is systematically skewed towards certain social categories.*

More recently, Baroness Warsi (BBC News Online, 2011) entered the debate concerning the rise in Islamophobia and a BBC headline declared: 'Baroness Warsi says Muslim prejudice seen as normal'.

The bulletin reported that the Baroness, the co-chairman of the Conservative Party, would discuss the issue during the speech at Leicester University: 'Prejudice against Muslims has "passed the dinner-table test" and become socially acceptable in the UK'. The statement is obviously sensational, but infers the processes of hegemony in practice, as prejudice against Muslims is appointed as a sense of normality.

When legitimate journalistic sources begin to add to the alarmist perspective and rhetoric, the stakes and challenges for working for a more open and inclusive society become even greater. For example Charles Moore, an editor of *The Spectator*, is quoted in the Runnymede Trust's (1997, page 9) report, writing in 1991:

> *You can be British without speaking English or being Christian or being white, but nevertheless Britain is basically English-speaking, Christian and white, and if one starts to think that it might become basically Urdu-speaking and Muslim and brown, one gets frightened and angry... Because of our obstinate refusal to have enough babies, Western European civilisation will start to die at the point when it could have been revived with new blood. Then the hooded hordes will win, and the Koran will be taught, as Gibbon famously imagined, in the schools of Oxford.*

ACTIVITY 5.3

Consider the quote by Charles Moore above and think about and, if possible, discuss the following two questions:

1) What stereotypes of Muslims and Islam are invoked by him?

2) What fears does he raise?

Think about what knowledge and understanding you would need to explore the statement above with young people you work with, to encourage more 'open' views of Islam and Muslims.

Sanghera and Bjorkert (2007) undertook research with 54 young men and women in Bradford between July 2004 and May 2005 and, in line with the earlier work of Lewis (2002), found that an assertive identity among Asian young Muslims was emerging. Reflecting on their own and the work of Lewis (2002), they state:

> *For Lewis (2002) an 'assertive Muslim identity' has emerged in Bradford that impacts negatively on women and minorities deemed 'outsiders' living within their territory. Such observations draw on what he describes as 'Muslim comfort zones' that have become closed and in which relatively large groups of Pakistani Muslim disaffected youth (particularly young males) are no longer in the control of the family and mosque, and have become increasingly alienated from their own political and community leaders. Although this assertive identity has been understood in relation to educational underachievement among young Pakistani Muslim men, Lewis suggests that it also has its roots in increasing Islamophobia, territoriality, gang formation and anti-social behaviour (including criminality). Religion as a cultural resource is central in the construction of an assertive identity.*

> (Sanghera and Bjorkert, 2007, pages 179–180)

Islam, with its existing notion of 'ummah' (brotherhood – see Modood et al., 1992; Sanghera and Bjorkert, 2007) provides a very handy hook to bring together other-wise diverse groups of young people. So, cultural dynamics internal to the Muslim communities of Britain and external hostility help create a force, which appears united and even homogeneous to outsiders. In fact, it masks a myriad of differ-ences based, for example, on the Sunni/Shiite allegiances and difficulties faced, especially, by the young people within those communities.

The rise in Islamophobia adds to the plethora of other issues faced by young Muslims in British society making them and their circumstances and also attitudes towards them an important focal point for all social care practitioners in society, including youth and dommunity workers. Hamid provides a useful time-frame to the changes in and relating to the current situation faced by young Muslims in Britain:

> *From the end of the 1980s to the early 21st Century, British Muslims have become a much more of a visible minority. Important developments have taken place in their communities as a result of changing demographics, social marginalisation, increasing religious awareness and the repercussions of local and international events. Young people have been instrumental in shaping some of these socio-political transformations. While many are well integrated and have gone on to become successful adults, an increasing number face a range of challenges which inhibit their opportunities and quality of life. This long list includes poor and overcrowded housing, educational underachievement, unemployment, a lack of parent-child communication, racism, Islamophobia, cultural alienation and increasing social problems such as: substance addiction, rise in criminal, anti-social behaviour and gang*

violence, teenage pregnancies, mental health problems and lack of political representation.

(Hamid, 2006, page 81)

Islamophobia includes within it prejudice, discrimination (both overt and covert) and is maintained and exercised especially through systematic media-based hegemony. It is clearly wrong and needs to be addressed, which is only possible if people acknowledge its existence. However, Jonathan Roberts (2006, page 28), when reflecting on his participation in the National Conference in Muslim youth work, which took place in Birmingham in December 2005, makes an interesting and important observation, when he points out:

The public data is readily available (NS 2006) that shows the current age profile of the Muslim population in the UK as 'the youngest age profile of all religious groups in Great Britain' (NS, 2006: Age and Sex). The 2001 census reported 535,853 Muslims between 0 and 16, in a Muslim population of 1,588,890, this is about 33.72% of the Muslim population, of whom 71% are under 34. This compares with a national population of 11,460,801 between 0 and 16, in a total population of 57,103,927, this is about 20.07% of the whole population, of whom 45% are under 34. Certainly, the Muslim population as a whole makes up 'only' 2.78% of the population, but when we look at the younger cohort of 0–16 year olds it makes up 4.6%: almost twice as significant to the development of the 'Every Child Matters' policy. The National Statistics summary of the UK population is that 1 in 5 are under 16 and 1 in 6 are over 65 and many of our public policies reflect this aging population. For the British Muslim population the profile is more like the UK in the 19th Century: 1 in 3 is under 16 and 1 in 25 over 65.

Therefore with the largest youth population, which is becoming identified as one of the most deprived and alienated from British society at large and which, according to other researchers (Lewis, 2004; Sanghera and Bjorkert, 2007), seems to be no longer in the control of the family and mosque (Sanghera and Bjorkert, 2007), the Muslim youth population of Britain needs some serious attention, starting with an understanding of their circumstances and legitimate grievances. Youth and community workers by virtue of their role and approach to young people (discussed in the last chapter) are well placed to take up this challenge. In fact, it is imperative they do so, because as Roberts goes on to remind us:

The Muslim population in the UK experiences the highest rate of unemployment: 14% for men and 15% for women in contrast to 4% of Christian men and women, and between 5% and 11% for other religious groups (NS, 2006: Labour Market). The Muslim population in the UK experiences the highest rate of ill health: 13% for men and 16% for women in contrast to 7–8% for Christian men and women (NS, 2006: Health and Disability). The Muslim population in the UK experiences the highest proportion of having no qualifications: 31% in contrast to 15% for Christians

(NS, 2006: Education). These statistics reveal a strong form of multiple deprivation in the British Muslim community that shows how they are 'cut off from the prosperity and opportunities that most of us take for granted' (Tony Blair in SEU, 2001:5).

(Roberts, 2006, page 28)

In such circumstances that clearly include unacceptable levels of deprivation, hostility from those outside the community, a lack of real cohesion within the Muslim community (in spite of perceptions which perhaps suggest the converse) and the possible attraction of ready-made 'masculine' identities which particularly provide a convenient means of uniting some young Muslims under the guise of protecting their religion, it is not surprising that notions of religious pride and honour are triggered (Soni, 2006). I had these sets of circumstances in mind when I came across an article in *The Guardian*, written by O'Hara (2011), focussing on the 'Sharp Increase in Suicide Rates in Northern Ireland', where she states:

Suicide rates have been rising markedly in Northern Ireland over the past decade. According to the Public Health Agency (PHA), after a period of relatively static figures in the latter half of the last century, between 1999 and 2008 rates of suicide in Northern Ireland increased by 64%. Most of the rise was attributable to young men in the 15 to 34 age group. A large proportion was concentrated in disadvantaged areas and, in particular, north and west Belfast.

The possible link between the rise in suicide rates and deprivation clearly has echoes in the circumstances and situation faced by young Muslims in Britain currently. However, one of the other factors that struck me in this article is,

Theories being mooted within Northern Ireland include the long-term impact of entrenched deprivation in some communities when coupled with issues of identity in a 'poor conflict' society and the legacy of the Troubles for some of the young generation of men and boys

(O'Hara, 2011)

More interestingly, O'Hara goes on to quote a Samaritans trustee, Stephen Platt, a Professor of Public Policy Research at the University of Edinburgh, who states:

The suicide rate in Northern Ireland appears to have increased after the end of the period known as the Troubles. Previous studies have shown that suicides decrease during periods of war because people feel a sense of integration in their communities while uniting against an adversary. When war ends, this feeling falls away to the detriment of mental health.

Suicide rates can also be affected by a number of different things including recession, rising employment, budget cuts and other social factors.

(Stephen Platt, cited by O'Hara, 2011)

In the current climate of the global recession, with well publicised budget cuts affecting British society, levels of deprivation affecting Muslim communities in Britain, the parallels with Northern Ireland, are clear. Perhaps even more disturbing is the fact that the rise in Islamophobia provides an unfortunate external force, which polarises especially young Muslim men from the perpetrators of Islamophobia and, therefore, provides the 'sense of integration' and also 'an adversary' to unite against. It is therefore unsurprising that as Parekh (2000) has also suggested, young Muslims are closing ranks when under external attack through the rise in Islamophobia. As I have suggested earlier, this is perhaps particularly significant given that Muslim cultures encourage the concept of 'ummah' (brotherhood).

Although there is little evidence of a rise in suicide rates among young Muslim men, it is significant and worrying that Sheridan, in her research, found that:

> More than one third of participants (35.6%) scored 4 or more on the GHQ-12, indicating the likely presence of mental ill health. What is not known is whether this ill health was wholly, in part, or not at all because of events that followed the September 11th terrorist attacks... Although causation may not be assumed, it would seem reasonable to infer that an abusive incident, particularly when coupled with a general upsurge in both implicit and overt discrimination, could lead to depressive symptoms.

> (2006, pages 333–334)

Clearly, more research needs to be undertaken in relation to this, but if the Northern Ireland example is indicative, then this is a worrying yet unsurprising development.

The Runnymede Trust's (1997) report on *British Muslims and Islamophobia* provides a useful, visual summary of the effects of Islamophobia on Muslims living as members of British society:

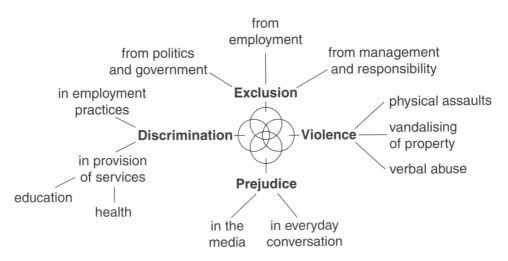

Figure 5.2 Islamophobia, a visual summary. The Runnymede Trust (1997, page 11). Reproduced with permission.

It is not difficult to see how Young's (1990) five faces of oppression (discussed in an earlier chapter) become a means by which the oppression of Muslim communities in Britain is exercised. It is not difficult to see how such communities, given the levels of deprivation, could become prone to exploitation, marginalisation, experience a lack of voice and therefore experience powerlessness, which can result in becoming powerless particularly in the face of the cultural imperialism displayed through the media. The fifth face of oppression, violence, is obvious, given the rise in racial attacks experienced by members of the Muslim communities in Britain.

ACTIVITY **5.4**

On 20 January 2008 the Observer Magazine *featured an article by Jason Burke, an 'Al-Qaeda expert', on 'The Britons Who Became Bombers'. The following is a small excerpt from the article (pages 16–17). Read it carefully and think about and list the possible 'push' factors and 'pull' factors that may influence young Muslim men like Ahmed and Mohammed into becoming suicide bombers.*

If possible, discuss your thoughts with another person or with a small group.

Mohammed and Ahmed, 17 and 19 respectively, are standing at a grubby bus stop on a high street in east London. It is an early Friday evening and they are talking about what to do later. The options are limited: play pool, hang about the estate, smoke some cannabis, watch DVDs, go for a drive in a friend's not-exactly stolen car. They have not been to Friday prayers at the local mosque for a long time, since they stopped going with their fathers, 'too much hassle, too many old men'. And they like a drink. Mohammed, who is wearing a fake gold necklace with the traditional Muslim hand of Fatima dangling from it, says his interests are 'films, music and cars'.

'And girls,' adds Ahmed.

Both men have been to Pakistan, to the Mirpur area of southern Kashmir, from where their parents, like most British Pakistani migrants, came 35 years ago. They did not like it much. 'Too hot and the food was rubbish and everything was dirty,' says Mohammed. Ahmed says, he had diarrhoea all the time he was there. 'Came back two stone lighter,' he jokes. As for politics, 'It's all lies,' says Mohammed. So what might turn Ahmed and Mohammed into suicide bombers? British intelligence analysts now talk of 'push factors' – those that make an individual more susceptible to radicalisation – and 'pull' factors – the actions of a recruiting agent that encourage someone towards violent activism. Analysts believe that many push factors are linked to the kind of identity problems common to second- or third-generation immigrants.

www.guardian.co.uk/theobserver/2008/jan/20/features.magazine77

The challenge for youth and community practice

What is clear from the previous discussion is that the challenges posed by the rise in Islamophobia are huge. Work needs to be undertaken both with Muslim and non-Muslim young people, across many communities. Most significantly, practitioners need to develop greater understanding of how Islamophobia operates, both in its subtle, 'normalised' guise and in its overtly discriminatory way. A 'subtle' example includes a teacher in a classroom, which included some Somalian children, saying to two little boys, who were clearly not paying attention and were chatting away to each other:

'Don't speak Somali here.'

The gulf that Islamophobia continues to create between communities requires practice in the building of trusting relationships (as discussed in the previous chapter).

It also requires confidence to engage with the issue and the situation it has created, needing practitioners to facilitate discussion and dialogue on a difficult subject. As Khan (2006, page 5), when addressing fellow youth workers in his introduction to the special edition of Youth and Policy on Muslim Youth titled 'Responding to Lives not Events', suggests: 'there is an absence or lack of acknowledgement given to conversations taking place by the professional enterprise that you are committed to and believe in?' He goes on to ask:

> *What happens when what you experience or see is rarely represented in the professional domain? ... What are the effects of the constant vilification of who you are on the self-esteem of Muslim young people in Britain? This absence of representation may be argued as legitimate due to capacity, but ultimately the narrative, and perspective presented is a matter of choice.*
>
> *(Khan, 2006, page 5)*

Indeed, failure to make the right choice may mean that practitioners, in fact, condone the hegemonic processes that lead to Islamophobia, rather than challenge them. Challenging 'them', to use Gramsci's (1971) model requires sustained education, nurturing understanding and taking action through the building of alliances (both, with and beyond Muslim communities), to bring about a real challenge and change to the status quo in regard to the circumstances created by Islamophobia. A good starting place would surely be the 'stock' of youth and community practice – nurturing conversations and dialogue and developing positive, trusting relationships.

C H A P T E R   R E V I E W

This chapter explored the nature of Islamophobia, examined the reasons for its existence and its rise in current British society. It poses challenges for both its victims and the practitioners.

In doing so, the chapter demonstrated how prejudice, stereotyping, othering, oppression and hegemony all operate in relation to the issue of Islamophobia.

Perhaps current attitudes to Islam, Muslim communities and the rise in Islamophobia pose many questions and challenges for each of us. As youth and community practitioners working with young people from Muslim and other communities, we are influenced to be both knowingly and unknowingly prejudiced. When attitudes are inevitably shaped through so many media discussed briefly in this chapter, it is perhaps natural to question and doubt ourselves. Indeed, as Davies points out, this is in fact fundamental to our practice:

For in the end, the process of applying our values and beliefs, including ones that are most deeply felt, requires judgement. And this in turn assumes questioning, the avoidance of the arrogance of certainty – an exploration of alternative interpretations and possibilities. In these processes doubt acts as a crucial safety valve.

(2006, page 73)

FURTHER READING

Chapter 2 on 'Islamophobia' from the Runnymede Commission on British Muslims and Islamophobia, by the Runnymede Trust (1997)

This chapter demonstrates how 'closed' views of Islam and Muslims are shaped through academic and journalistic writing and the media in general.

Davies, B (2006) The Place of Doubt in Youth Work – A Personal Journey, *Youth and Policy*, no. 92, Summer 2006. NYA, Leicester.

Bernard Davies reflects with brutal honesty on his reflections on participating at a conference – Youth Work in Bradford – as a white male, and especially 'western'.

Chapter 6

The challenge of globalisation

Introduction

I hope that reading this book, with its six key chapters, has taken you on a journey of self-reflection and learning. We started with a focus on the self, and this final chapter now considers the self in the context of the much wider global world.

When I have discussed the inclusion of a chapter on globalisation in the context of cross-cultural studies/dynamics or working with diversity, often, people (including students) have expressed surprise. They often ask, 'Why is knowledge and understanding of globalisation and the global context important for youth and community practice, when the practice is often in diverse but small-scale local contexts?'

The response to this important question has three elements.

1. The first concern, the inescapable fact about youth and community practice in regard to its key tenets of active participation, education and empowerment all underpinned by principles of equality and equity, is that these are designed to ensure that in applying these principles in practice, practitioners are hopefully engaged in processes that enable young people to make informed choices. My point is that if practitioners are to truly enable young people to make informed choices, then they must understand what affects them in their lives. This has to include both an understanding of their immediate circumstances (such as those related to their home/community-based lives) and the wider influences that impact their lives, including the forces of globalisation. These wider, global forces, in fact, fundamentally affect each of us in today's globalised world. As Kofi Annan, a former General Secretary of the United Nations, is once reported to have said,

   It has been said that arguing against globalisation is like arguing against the law.

Therefore, if young people are to be supported by youth and community workers in making informed choices, then an understanding and knowledge of the global world and the forces of globalisation is essential.

2. In relation to the second element of the above question, the reality of a globalised world means that there are inequalities in relation to the distribution of and access to power and resources in local communities, because of the globalised nature of the world we live in, which inevitably affects people on the grounds of their race, ethnicity, gender, sexuality, disability etc. Thus, the other inescapable fact about the globalised world is its relationship with difference and diversity.

3. The third element, also linked to the notion of the globalised world and the diversity of people and cultures that live within it, is the concern with the future, or more accurately, with ensuring that we maintain and develop resources which can and will sustain the future generations that will inhabit the earth. Therefore, concerns with concepts of sustainability and sustainable development have to be considered in the context of a globalised world.

This chapter therefore is very important concerning the book as a whole. It will begin by exploring the concept and effects of globalisation and then move on to look at sustainable development. The significance of interdependence as an underpinning aspect of both globalisation and sustainable development will then be examined. It will then focus on globalisation and its relationship with power, equality and inequality in the world. Finally, youth and community work's response to the globalised context in which young people inevitably exist will be explored by focusing on global youth work practice.

It is important to point out at this early stage that I am not an economist and the knowledge and perspective presented in this chapter is what can be described as a 'lay' person's perspective, but it is one that has real importance for youth and community practitioners.

Understanding globalisation

Globalisation is a complex concept and has many different facets within it. Held and McGrew help to nurture an understanding of it when they state:

No single universally agreed definition of globalisation exists. As with all core concepts in the social sciences, its precise meaning remains contested. Globalisation has been variously conceived as action at a distance (whereby the actions of social agents in the locale can come to have significant consequences for 'distant others'); time-space compression (referring to the way in which instantaneous electronic communication erodes the constraints of distance and time on social organization and interaction); accelerating interdependence (understood as the intensification of enmeshment among national economics and societies, such that events in one country impact directly on others): a shrinking world (the erosion of borders and geographical barriers to socio-economic activity); and, among other concepts, global integration, the reordering of inter-regional power relations, consciousness of the global condition, and the intensification of inter-regional connectedness.

(2000, page 3)

ACTIVITY **6.1**

Some of the key elements, from the definition of globalisation by Held and McGrew, are listed below. Can you think of an example for each of the aspects of globalisation listed? You may need to study the definition once again before completing this activity.

- *action at a distance*
- *time-space compression*
- *accelerating inter-dependence*
- *a shrinking world*

The development and advancement in technology and economic infrastructures, has meant that the idea: 'the actions of social agents in the locale can come to have significant consequences for distant others' (Held and McGrew, 2000, page 3), is very real for people living in communities around the world. As a resident of Birmingham, for example, the demise of the Rover car industry has had a huge impact on the workers from the numerous communities of Birmingham, and especially of Longbridge, who were employed there in their thousands. The assurance that one generation of workers may be followed by their sons and daughters led to all the real-life consequences experienced by those who face an uncertain future. The industry is a shadow of its former nationalised self, with Chinese and Indian interests now playing a part in it.

This aspect of globalisation underpinned and made possible by the way in which instantaneous electronic communications erode 'the constraints of distance and time on social organisation and interaction' (Held and McGrew, 2000, page 3), especially in regard to the movement of finance and other economic resources, means that globalisation in this guise is a reality for all of us. When you visit another country, for example, you may take the ability to use your credit card for granted, but this is actually only possible because of globalisation.

For those residents of Birmingham still employed in its Chinese or Indian business controlled industries, the reality of the interconnected world is very obvious.

The significance of such developments to bring about changes in the local and global contexts must not be underestimated and, more importantly, must be understood. At the 1999 TUC Congress in Brighton the then Secretary of State for International Development pointed out:

> *I often say that globalisation is as big an historical shift as was the change from feudalism to industrialisation. That earlier shift remade the whole political and economic landscape of the world. It brought economic growth, but unequal benefits. And it gave birth to the trade union movement.*

> (Short, 1999, page 4)

Clare Short's reference at the end of the quote above to the trade union movement, which was responsible for campaigning and negotiating for greater equality and better pay and conditions for workers, is important and must be remembered. She is clearly hinting that the present legacy being created by the forces of globalisation will require a significant organisation for collective action, to ensure that the principles of equality and equity are protected and implemented in the present circumstances created by globalisation.

The processes of globalisation discussed above have become an inevitable aspect of the world. The fact that resources (financial and others) can be moved so quickly around the world and that the development of telecommunications networks enable almost instant communication across huge distances bring obvious advantages. However, unless these processes are guided by ethical practices, the disadvantages become obvious and relate particularly to the dangers of a profit driven ethos, which may over-ride any humanitarian concerns, issues of social justice and sustainability.

King (1999, page 399) summarises the key effects or elements of globalisation, while also sounding a warning in relation to the diversity of cultures in the world:

> *The immense acceleration on the process of globalisation and 'global compression' is most obviously seen in relation to the economy: the three major players in the internationalisation of the economy since the 1970s,*

> *have been the banks, the global corporations and the state (Thrift, 1986);*
> *it has been accompanied by the internationalisation of production and of*
> *consumption, of twenty-four hour global trading in securities, of revolutionary*
> *developments in transport and telecommunication technology, and the*
> *massive growth in international labour migration. These in turn have brought*
> *the deterritorialization of cultures, the existence of cultures far from their*
> *places of origin.*

This latter point made by King has some obvious resonance with my life, especially given that I live as a Hindu woman of Indian descent in British society and have never really lived in India. I have visited the country whose religion and cultures I lay some claim to, but never really lived there. However, my story pre-dates the period of 'acceleration' in the movement of people and their cultures, the processes of acclimatising to a new environment or society are no longer at a slow, gradual pace, which enabled people like me to make sense of the changes and differences (especially in relation to culture) that I encountered in my life. Now, the process can be aided by undertaking prior research using the internet, but surely, this is not enough to prepare your senses fully to the onslaught of likely new experiences and potential differences that you will experience at a much faster pace?

In relation to how the internet in particular, alongside other audio-visual sources, is shaping perceptions of other cultures was conveyed to me during an encounter with a young man while travelling on the Delhi Metro. He struck up a conversation with my husband and me as we headed off on the same Metro Line. He was keen to complete the usual pleasantries such as 'Where are you from?', and then moved quickly on to asking what appeared to be quite 'strange' questions. These included:

> *Where do your young people meet in England?*
> *Can young women go out at night?*
> *How safe is it?*

He then said, *This is the first time I have had the chance to ask these questions directly to someone who actually lives there – otherwise we only see things through films and on the internet, even though I work for a big corporation.*

The ways in which large corporations are interacting with and influencing local cultures are also interesting. For example, on a visit to Bangalore (in India), a couple of years ago, as I arrived in the middle of the night at 3am at a friend's home, I noticed a number of mini-buses trundling along the otherwise deserted street. The next day the friend I was staying with explained how these mini-buses were used every night to pick up young men and women, who were working in the call centres of some international corporations. When you're sitting in the comfort of your own home, ringing a help desk, and someone with a slight Indian lilt, masked often by an American accent, answers the phone, it is difficult to imagine that this person is in fact working through the night in a part of the world which is at least four hours ahead of you. My friend's comments were striking:

They get really good money for India Sangeeta, but it is playing havoc with the lives of families. Parents have no idea what to think about it – especially where the young women are concerned. On the one hand, they earn good money to support the household, but on the other, it's going completely against family traditions and family life. It can cause real conflict, because the young people can be fashionable and enjoy the things that a few years ago they could only imagine – especially 'Western' goods, but the parents feel unsure and don't understand what is really happening.

My friend works as a Christian Minister and had encountered many incidents of such conflict in her pastoral role with members of her congregation. The fact that she highlighted how India's young people seem to aspire to acquire Western goods (including dress) is another consequence of globalisation's impact on traditional cultures. On a visit to a trendy shopping mall in Delhi recently, I found it both surprising and comical, that most of the clothes shops (the equivalent of big department stores or clothes fashion chains in the West) sold mainly Western clothes (such as jeans and t-shirts), but had sections titled 'ethnic clothing'. As I ventured into these parts of the stores, I found the traditional Indian clothing, (Punjabi suits, shalwar-kameez, saris) there. So, home-designed, produced, traditional clothes were now being considered 'ethnic'. However sad this seemed, it is the homogenising affects of globalisation that is a real threat to diversity and traditional cultural practices. The mall housed at least three fast-food chains, including Papa Johns, MacDonalds and Pizza Hut – an indication of how other aspects of traditional Indian culture are perhaps being rejected in preference to such outlets. Ritzer (2000) aptly captured this process of homogenisation in his book, 'The McDonaldization of Society'.

Sustainable development

It seems that whether those involved in the processes of globalisation are mindful of the significance of sustainable development, will determine the extent to which the world becomes increasingly unequal or becomes more conscious of sharing the prosperity generated through the benefits of globalisation. The Brundtland Commission (1987, page 43) stated that:

Sustainable development is development that meets the needs of the present, without compromising the ability of future generations to meet their own needs.

Therefore, sustainability is about ensuring that the present inhabitants of the earth look after it in a way that ensures that the needs of future generations will and can be met. In relation to this, two key elements emerge as fundamental – the first concerns the recognition that in spite of growing wealth development, there are still millions who live in poverty, which means the present needs are not being met. The second aspect relates to the notion of resources, which inevitably engenders concern with existing environmental resources, which should be maintained and not depleted, and left in a state which protects them (from, for example, pollution) for the use of future generation. As Barbier points out:

> *The primary objective of Sustainable Development is to reduce the absolute poverty of the world's poor through providing lasting and secure livelihoods that minimize resource depletion, environmental degradation, cultural disruption and social instability.*

(1987, page 101)

Therefore, in simple terms, sustainable development is about living within limits, understanding the interconnections between the social, economic, political and environmental aspects of our lives, which in turn are influenced by the processes of globalisation. It is also about the equitable distribution of resources and opportunities. None of these aspects of sustainable development should be particularly alien to youth and community principles and practice, yet it is rare to come across practitioners who engage with these concepts – the exceptions are those who are employed specifically to raise awareness of them (such as environmental youth workers and global youth workers).

Essentially, the agenda for both sustainable development and youth and community practice is very similar. Both are concerned with people and in particular with processes of active participation, education and empowerment and addressing issues of poverty, to improve the quality of people's lives, which in turn concerns issues of power and resource distribution. Both are also concerned with the notion of continuity in the face of change and with the future; and in pursuing these, both have to address the environmental implications and raise awareness, so that people take responsibility and make informed choices.

Clare Short provided a useful link between globalisation and the concerns of sustainable development:

> *Today, globalisation is causing massive economic and social change. Huge wealth is being created, but we are also seeing an enormous growth in inequality, between countries and within countries. The challenge of our times is to ensure that the wealth and opportunity generated by globalisation is distributed equitably; and that we seize the opportunity for a rapid period of advance and a reduction in the suffering caused by poverty worldwide.*

(1999, page 2)

This is both the biggest moral challenge our generation faces and a growing challenge to our own interests. If we do not reduce poverty, the conflict, disease and environmental degradation to which it leads, will damage the prospects of the next generation, wherever they live.

Interdepedence

The concept of interdependence links both globalisation and sustainable development, and is an integral element in both. At its simplest, it is about the connections that people have with each other and the dependence/reliance they have on each other, either directly or through the production and consumption of goods. Short (1999, page 5) states:

> *Global economic integration and interdependence is a reality. We cannot turn back the clock. Our common challenge is to manage the globalisation process equitably and sustainably.*

The following activity may help you to understand the extent to which interdependence is a part of our lives.

ACTIVITY **6.2**

Think of waking up, getting dressed, having breakfast and taking a journey (for example, to work or to visit someone) one morning. Then make a list of all the things/items that played a part in this process (such as the clothes you wore, the cereal you ate, the fruit or yoghurt you may have had as a part of your breakfast, the petrol or diesel you may have used in travelling etc.). On this particular morning, pay some attention to where these items were made and/or produced and alongside the list of items, write down where they may have come from.

This is a very simple way of understanding how our lives are enmeshed with the lives of others, perhaps a long way from us, but we never really think about this – we tend to take it for granted. However, the very things we take for granted may in fact be the result of oppression, through exploitation and marginalisation of others (Young, 1990).

ACTIVITY **6.3**

The case study that follows is written by Paedar Cremin and taken from a book called Rethinking Globalization *(edited by Bigelow and Peterson, 2002). It is a very sad but true story and demonstrates how exploitation takes place through processes of globalisation.*

Read the case study carefully and then think very deeply about the question posed: 'Who Killed Iqbal Masih?'

Also consider the chain of events that led to his death. Ultimately who had power in this situation, and why?

CASE STUDY: WHO KILLED IQBAL MASIH?

> *No one shall be held in slavery or servitude; slavery and the slave trade shall be prohibited in all their forms.*
>
>   *(The United Nations Universal Declaration of Human Rights, Article 4)*

Iqbal Masih lived in the village of Muridka in Pakistan. His family was extremely poor and lived in a two-roomed hut.

When Iqbal was four years old, his family was given a loan of 800 rupees (about £16.00) in return for putting Iqbal to work in the village carpet factory. Around 500,000 children aged between 4 and 14 work in carpet factories in Pakistan. They are considered good workers. They work for 14 hours a day. Their small hands are good for tying the knots of expensive hand-knotted carpets.

These child workers receive no formal education. They are not allowed to speak during working time, in case they make mistakes in the patterns. They have one 30 minute lunch break per day, and often are forced to work overtime without extra pay. Complaints result in beatings, having their fingers plunged into boiling water or other punishments.

Iqbal was extremely unhappy at the carpet factory, but his parents could not afford to have him set free. One day, in 1992, Iqbal heard the founder of the Bonded Labour Liberation Front (BLLF) speak about their work in freeing bonded labourers and about new laws, which forbade child labour. Iqbal asked how he could be set free. He knew that the factory owner claimed that his parents now owed 16,000 rupees. He was afraid his entire life would be spent repaying the debt. He wanted to have a childhood like other children.

When Iqbal returned to the factory, he told the owner of his rights under the law, and stated that he would no longer work as a slave. The carpet-master was furious and punished him severely, but still the child refused to work. Iqbal said 'I am not afraid of the carpet-master. He should be afraid of me'. The factory owner demanded his worker or his money. The family could not convince Iqbal to work and so the factory owner threatened them. The family had to flee from their village. Iqbal was taken by the BLLF to a school which they had in Lahore. He was ten years of age and he worked very hard, quickly learning to read and write. He hoped that one day he could become a lawyer, helping to free child labourers.

In 1993, when he was eleven, Iqbal began to work with the BLLF. He sneaked into factories to see where the child labourers were kept. He began to make speeches at the factory gates, telling the workers of their rights. As a result, 3000 child labourers broke away from their masters, and thousands of adults began to demand improved working conditions. In 1993 and 1994, people in the West learned about Iqbal's work. They began to ask questions about carpet production in Pakistan. Carpet exports fell for the first time in three decades. The manufacturers and exporters blamed Iqbal Masih for the problems in their industry. In 1994, Iqbal was given a number of human rights awards and invitations to visit a number of Western countries. Doctors in Sweden found that he was the size of a child half his age. He suffered from tuberculosis, and various vascular and pulmonary problems. His spine was curved, his fingers bent by arthritis. Malnutrition and abuse had left him physically maimed.

On his return from his triumphant visit to the West, Iqbal found that the BLLF was in trouble. Threats of violence had been made against the BLLF's workers and teachers. The government was involved in investigating BLLF's staff. The carpet factory owners were planning to challenge the work of the organisation.

In April 1995, Iqbal went on a visit to Muridike, to see some members of his family. As he travelled with a cousin through fields near the village, a shot rang out, and Iqbal Masih fell dead. A poor labourer called Muhammad Ashrat at first confessed to the killing, but later withdrew his confession. International pressure has failed to get any satisfactory answer as to why Iqbal Masih, aged 13, died.

This case study facilitates understanding of the complex issues surrounding globalisation and sustainable development and the links to ethical, moral judgements and actions, which in turn underpin the decisions we make, the level of responsibility we take and most importantly, the choices we make once we know the true picture.

When I first became involved with projects in Tamil Nadu (south India) that worked with child labourers in the matchstick-making industry and those who worked as 'rag' pickers, I became very emotional and motivated, but also came up with what now seems like solutions that were poorly thought through:

'The answer lies, obviously, in better education', I said to my colleagues in Indian local non-governmental organisations (local charities). Their response was usually to the point:

> *It is not as simple as that, Sangeeta. If you take the children out of the industry, then the family loses an essential part of its income that helps it to survive. The bosses in the industry get 'nasty' and start to threaten the families. The parents' immediate concern is how to feed the family on a daily basis – education and schools are a long way from that. The education should start with the hoteliers, who have the power to make a more responsible choice, and therefore can stop using 'child-labour' produced match sticks in their hotels. Education and awareness amongst the tourists and business people would also help – if only they would stop staying in hotels that obviously use child labour, not only for match sticks, but also in their kitchens and restaurants. Child labour in India is illegal, but is going on all around us. But starting just with the child and the family is not exactly the answer.*

The experiences I have had in such situations have always been invaluable and instructive – you really need to know, appreciate and understand the full picture.

There are so many connections between people and goods, across many different levels, which add to the complexity. As Hannerz (1999, page 7) points out:

> *...the world has become one network of social relationships, and between its different regions, there is a flow of meanings as well as of people and goods.*

The 'politics' of globalisation: inequality and social justice

One of the key effects of the acceleration in the processes of globalisation is the development of huge corporations that are driven mainly by capitalist principles of profit-generation. Their size and expansion poses a threat to smaller-scale, local enterprises that cannot compete with them and has a real impact on local economies and cultures. You only have to think about the local corner shop and its demise in Britain, in the wake of the development and expansion of huge supermarket chains, to appreciate the change that this entails. The multi-nationals therefore have huge sway and power, given their size, authority and wealth. In fact, not only do they pose a threat to smaller businesses but also are a threat to some nations. Anthony D. Smith states:

> *Broadly speaking, it is argued that the era of the nation-state is over. We are entering a new world of economic giants and superpowers of multinationals and military blocs, of vast communications networks and international division of labour. In such a world, there is no room for medium or small-scale states, let alone submerged ethnic communities and their competing and their devisive nationalisms. On the one hand, capitalist competition has given birth to immensely powerful transnational corporations with huge budgets, reserves of skilled labour, advanced technologies and sophisticated information networks. Essential to their success is the ability to deliver suitably packaged imagery and symbolism, which will convey their definitions of the services they provide. While they have to rely on a transnational lingua franca, it is the new systems of telecommunications and computerized information networks, which enable them to by-pass differences in language and culture, to secure the labour and markets they require. In other words, the resources, range and specialized flexibility of transnational corporations' activities enable them to present imagery and information on an almost global scale, threatening to swamp the cultural networks of more local units, including nations and ethnic communities.*

> (Smith, 1990, page 174)

The fact however is that although these organisations provide employment for millions of people around the world, on the whole, the real wealth and control lies in the hands of the few that own and manage these enterprises. As Pilger (2001, pages 1 and 2) points out:

> *The facts of globalisation are revealing, a small group of powerful individuals are now richer than most of the population of Africa. Just 200 giant*

corporations dominate a quarter of the world's economic activity: General Motors is now bigger than Denmark, Ford is bigger than South Africa.

The fact is that such wealth has not just been created over a few years – there is a legacy and a history, often of exploitation on which it may have been built. It is the 'elites' of the world, who often already had existing power, wealth and resources that have been able to further benefit from the processes of globalisation. This means that there is a class-based and often also a racial context to the relationship between those with power, and those who are subject to it. Joseph et al. (2002, page 9), for example, suggest that:

> *The colonial legacy however, provides a crucial contextual framework for an understanding of the impact that globalisation has had on Black people, their political and economic status in the world today, their contribution to global society and their continued oppression and exploitation.*

They recognise that there is an important historical context on which present enterprises are built and from which they continue to benefit:

> *A Black perspective is not a single-issue political strategy. It recognises that the process of Western globalisation over the past five hundred years has not been a neutral process, and that it has imposed upon the world a cultural and political outlook that is sexist, racist, ageist, homophobic and exploitative of working people. The impact on the Black and majority world communities has been one of either reinforcing and legitimising existing inequalities or introducing new ones, where previously they did not exist.*

> (Joseph et al., 2002, pages 7 and 8)

The crude divide is between those with power and wealth and those without it. Unfortunately, the millions that are exploited to generate such wealth usually go unrecognised – the 'normal' fate of those that are marginalised and exploited (Young, 1990). As such, Pilger coined the term 'unpeople' to describe these masses. As Jones, writing in *The Guardian* in March 2011, explains the term,

> *... it refers to millions of people in poor countries, who are marginalised or entirely absent from media coverage. Because these people are a faceless mass, it's easy for Western governments to wage war against them. After all, if electorates can't imagine that there are real people suffering the consequences of war, they are less likely to protest.*

> (Jones, 2011)

ACTIVITY 6.4

This activity involves watching and listening to excerpts from John Pilger's documentary, The New Rulers of the World, which was broadcast on 13 July 2001.

ACTIVITY 6.4 *continued*

Although the focus of the documentary is on the impact of globalisation on Indonesia, the historical parallels with more 'current' developments (such as Iraq) are startling. So, when you watch and listen to the excerpts, keep Iraq in mind.

Click on the following link to access the excerpts: www.inminds.com/new-rulers-of-the-world.html

If possible, try and watch the full version of the documentary, which is available through John Pilger's web-site (www.johnpilger.com)

Also, think about the following questions:
* *What part did poverty play in the exploitation of workers?*
* *How can you apply the theory of 'hegemony' to the situation featured in the documentary concerning Indonesia?*

Pilger's (2001) documentary explored the unjust impact of the forces of globalisation, resulting in keeping millions in a state of poverty. It also demonstrated how hegemony (Gramsci, 1971) operates, to facilitate the processes of exploitation and marginalisation, both historically and in modern times. The effect on families, cultures and structures is devastating.

Youth and community practitioners need to recognise and understand the processes at work – only then can they help effectively challenge them and in the process, enable young people to make truly informed choices. In regard to the youth and community practitioner's commitment to moral and ethical practice and, therefore, to promote social justice, practitioners should be engaged in:

> *Education for sustainability [which] is the creation of a sense and practice of global citizenship in all humanity... It should be about consciousness raising and conscience pricking.*

> (O'Riordan cited by Bourn and McCollum, 1995, page 78)

Pilger's (1991) work is both an 'eye opener' and a 'conscience pricking' exercise.

Global youth work

Global Youth Work, a youth work process of working with young people that aims to enable them to make international links and to recognise the impact of the 'global on the local' and the 'local on the global', was formally established in the late 1990s. It was a response by youth workers to address the impact of globalisation and raise awareness among young people of its significance. In a 'Global Youth Work' pack (2007), available from the National Youth Agency, one of the editors, Momodou Sallah said: 'It will help make the personal, local, national and global connection between 'things out there' and 'things in here'.'

In the introduction to the pack, Sallah and joint-editor Sophie Cooper state:

> *Globalisation has become of increasing significance, as evidenced by the fact that Gordon Brown identified it as one of six priorities to build a 'stronger, fairer Britain'. It refers to the world coming together, due to closer economic, cultural, environmental, political and technological interactions, resulting in global interdependence.*

For youth and community workers, it is imperative that they appreciate the impact of forces at work in shaping young people's lives. They must have knowledge and understanding of the link between globalisation, sustainability, young people and their practice as Youth and Community Workers. I have tried to illustrate these dimensions in the diagram below. It is through developing an understanding of these concepts and their impact that effective global youth work can be undertaken.

Table 6.1 The link between globalisation, sustainability, young people and the youth and community worker

Globalisation	Young people and the youth and community worker	Sustainability
↓		↓
Profit driven		Concerned with community
↓		↓
	Needs, understanding + knowledge of both, to be able to fully understand contexts, circumstances, the distribution and effects of power on young people & their families	
↓		↓
Grand scale		Global/local context
↓		↓
Movement of people/money/ resources around the world affecting communities as producers and consumers & affecting the environment in relation to these processes		Concerned with the environment plus maintenance of resources for future generations
		↓
		Concerned with quality of life (connections between social, economic, political, environmental aspects of life)

As Short (1999, page 7) stated over a decade ago:

> *The challenge for the new Millennium is to advance these principles of social justice in a new, more interdependent world. To bring real advances in human welfare for millions of working people and their families.*

I believe that the challenge continues to be imperative.

C H A P T E R   R E V I E W

This chapter explored the concept of globalisation and its impact, and examined the importance of sustainable development and its relationship with globalisation. The principle of interdependence and its influence in all our lives was also discussed, before moving on to exploring the potential 'cost' of globalisation in relation to the principles of equality, equity and social justice.

In this regard, I made extensive use of case studies and the work of John Pilger, and in doing so, I hope I helped to nurture better awareness and understanding and demonstrated the potential cultural impact.

The chapter concluded with a focus on global youth work as a method that practitioners can use to raise awareness of the concepts discussed and the issues and circumstances created by them.

FURTHER READING

Friedman, J (1994) *Cultural Identity and Global Process*, London: Sage.

Although this is quite a dated text, two chapters are particularly relevant to some of the themes discussed in this chapter – Chapter 5 on Culture, Identity and World Process, and Chapter 7 on 'Globalization and Localization'.

Ritzer, G (2000) *The McDonaldization of Society*. London: Pine Forge Press.

This fascinating text that explores how the culture related to the fast-food industry permeates our society and therefore our lives.

Conclusion

The writing of this book has been a personal endeavour for me, in which I have committed to paper many personal and professional reflections, exercises created, planned and discussed with numerous others – colleagues and friends – over many years.

The intention from the beginning was to enable co-practitioners to think about who they are and how they behave and the impact and effect of this in the context of diversity, in its many guises. It was never intended to be a policy-maker's 'handbook' or critique of policies or the legal framework that underpins practice in regard to issues of equality. As important as I believe this tool is, there are others much more knowledgeable than me who have written about this eloquently and with great clarity and purpose.

In a sense, using the imagery of a 'circle', common in both Hinduism and Buddhism, I hoped to take the reader practitioner on a circular journey, starting in the first chapter with the self in relation to identity and culture and how these interact with each other, including encouraging reflections on identity in relation to those that are both similar and different from oneself. This hopefully captured the essence of working with diversity in practice right at the beginning of the journey.

The next two chapters were largely concerned with the 'business' of understanding the key concepts and theories that I believe deepen understanding of cross-cultural dynamics and/or working with diversity. As such, the second chapter aimed mainly to de-mystify the language and terminology of cross-cultural dynamics, while Chapter 3 focused on some significant theories and theorists whose work, I believe, facilitates understanding of dynamics and circumstances, created and existing in society, relating to working in a diverse context, including the impact and interplay of power and authority in relation to different cultural communities in any multi-cultural society.

The fourth chapter tackled two elements of 'practice', in relation to diversity, and especially in regard to differences that I believe are fundamental. The first of these related to the significance of 'trust' and the second advocated the importance of 'storying' as a tool in working with diversity and is made possible mainly by the development of positive, trusting relationships.

In Chapter 5, with the focus on the existence of and rise in Islamophobia in British and other Western societies, I tried to demonstrate the relevance of some of the concepts and theories discussed in earlier chapters. This chapter, perhaps more than any of the others so far, posed challenges for the practitioner in relation to the dynamics of difference, and I hope it also inferred a sense of urgency for youth and community practitioners to take action.

Finally, in Chapter 6, I explored the concepts of globalisation, sustainable development and interdependence and discussed the potential and resulting consequences of the forces of globalisation on young people and the cultures and societies to which they belong. I hope I managed to convey the significance of the global context in relation to localised lives and to demonstrate how such forces affect the balance of power and processes of equality, equity and social justice. I also aimed to explore the importance of using Global Youth Work as a means of raising awareness among young people about how global forces impact their lives, so that they can make truly informed decisions and choices.

Throughout this circular journey, the activities aimed to help the reader/practitioner to develop their knowledge and understanding and ultimately question their practice. The intention was never to deal in absolutes, but to encourage self-reflection, and more importantly, questioning. As Rumi, the early thirteenth century mystical poet, once said:

> The way leads through doubt to the shore of truth

> Just as an answer is reached through questioning

(Cited in Davies, 2006, page70)

Since the emphasis throughout this book has been on self-reflection and questioning, I would like to end this journey appropriately, with an activity, which I hope continues to make you reflect and question, and continues the metaphors of travellers and journeys that the book started with.

ACTIVITY 7.1

Read the story 'The Watermelon' from a book by Nick Owen (2001)

Once you have read the story carefully, think about the following questions:

a) Which of the two travellers do you think was right?

b) Why?

c) What would you have done in their situation? The same as either of them, or would you have done something different?

d) What do you think about the final statement (at the end of the story), made by the second traveller?

The watermelon

A traveller was crossing a broad and barren plain. He'd been travelling since morning, and now he was hot, tired and hungry. He watched the sun setting towards the mountains in the west, and began wondering where he might find a place to rest and somewhere to sleep that evening.

He reached the edge of the plain, and gazed down over a deep valley. Far in the distance, he could just make out a distant village, smoke from the chimneys curling lazily into the evening sky.

He urged his horse down the switchback track to the valley floor. He was already anticipating an ice cold drink to quench his thirst, the taste of local delicacies, and good companionship.

When he reached the edge of the village, it seemed deserted. There was just one street with houses and a few shops each side, but through the haze of evening, he could barely distinguish some kind of activity at the far end of the community.

Urging his horse forward, he realised all the villagers were gathered around a fence, which surrounded a field. As he drew closer, he could hear the nervous shouts of the people. When they saw him they pleaded, "Help us, Senor. Save us from the monster."

The traveller looked into the field. All he could see was a huge watermelon.

"Please save us, Senor. It's going to attack."

"That's not a monster. It's a watermelon. It's just a rather oversized fruit."

"It's a monster, and it's going to attack. Help us."

"It's a watermelon."

"It's a monster."

"It's a water..."

But before he could finish, the enraged villagers pulled him from his horse and threw him into the fishpond. Afterwards, they lashed him to his horse, and harried him out of the village.

An hour or so later, another traveller was following hard on the heels of the former. The sun was already lower in the west, and he was feeling even thirstier and hungrier than the first traveller. He too contemplated a drink and good honest food of the region.

He snaked down the side of the valley, and reached the outskirts of the village. He saw the crowd agitated and shouting by the fence.

"What's the problem?" he asked.

"Look, a fierce green monster. It's going to attack us."

"So there is," said the traveller. "It's big, and it's certainly fierce. Let me help you."

87

He drew his sword, spurred on his horse, leaped the fence, and in no time at all, bits of watermelon were flying everywhere. The villagers, covered in red slush, and black pips, were cheering and clapping. The traveller was carried in triumph through the village, and invited to stay as long as he wished.

They put him in the best room at the hotel, they paid all his expenses, they served him the best food and the best wines of the region. And in return, he took time to listen and learn about their culture, their history, their stories, their way of life.

And as he did so, little by little, he won the trust and confidence of these people. He began to tell them about his culture, his history, his stories, and the way of life of his own people. And very gently and delicately, he began to teach them the difference between a monster and a watermelon.

And so in the fullness of time, the villagers began to plant and cultivate watermelons in their fields. And when the time finally came for the traveller to leave, he passed by the field, now full of rows and rows of massive watermelons awaiting harvest. And a villager said, "Thank you so much, Senor. You have taught us many things. And you have shown us how to tame the watermelon, and make it work for us."

And the traveller said, "You indeed have fine watermelons. But always remember, even watermelons can sometimes be monsters."

Owen, N (2001) 'The Watermelon' from *The Magic of Metaphor: 77 Stories for Teachers, Trainers and Thinkers*. Carmarthen: Crown House Publishing Limited. www.crownhouse.co.uk. Reproduced with permission.

References

Allen, C (2005) From race to religion: The new face of discrimination, in Abbas, T (ed) *Muslim Britain: Communities Under Pressure*. London: Zed Books.

Allen, C and Neilsen, JS (2002) *Summary Report on Islamophobia in the EU After 11 September 2001*. Vienna: European Monitoring Centre on Racism and Xenophobia.

Anderson, B (1983) *Imagined Communities: Reflection on the Origins and Spread of Nationalism*. London: Verso.

Barbier, E (1987) The concept of sustainable economic development. *Environmental Conservation*, 14(2): 101–10.

Bar-Tel, D and Labin, D (2001) The effects of a major event on stereotyping: terrorist attacks in Israel and Israeli adolescents' perceptions of Palestinians, Jordanians and Arabs. *European Journal of Social Psychology,* **31**: 265–80.

BBC News Online (2011) *Politics: Baroness Warsi says Muslim Prejudice Seen as Normal*, BBC News Online 20 January 2011 **www.bbc.co.uk/news/uk-politics-12235237** (accessed 4 April 2011).

Bigelow, B and Peterson, B (2002) *Rethinking Globalization: Teaching for Justice in an Unjust World*. Milwaukee: Rethinking Schools Press.

Blakemore, K and Griggs, E (2007) *Social Policy: An Introduction*, 3rd edition. Maidenhead: McGraw Hill and Open University Press.

Bodley, JH (1997) *Cultural Anthropology: Tribes, States and the Global System*, Mountain View, CA: Mayfield Publishing Company.

Bourn, D and McCollum, A (1995) *A World of Difference: Making Global Connections in Youth Work*. London: Development Education Association.

Bowler, R (2010) Learning from lives, in Buchroth, I and Parkin, C (eds.) *Using Theory in Youth and Community Practice*. Exeter: Learning Matters.

Bulmer, M (1986) Race and ethnicity, in Burgess, RG (ed) *Key Variables in Social Investigation*. London: Routledge and Kegan Paul.

Brundtland Commission (WCED) Report (1987) *Our Common Future*. Oxford: Oxford University Press.

Burke, B (1999, 2005) Antonio Gramsci, Schooling and Education, the encyclopedia of informal education. Available online at **www.infed.org/thinkers/et-gram.htm**

Burke, J (2008) Omar was a normal British teenager who loved his little brother and Man Utd. So why at 24 did he plan to blow up a nightclub in central London? Available online at **www.guardian.co.uk/theobserver/2008/jan/20/features.magazine77** (c) Guardian News & Media Ltd 2008 (accessed 20 January 2008).

Cambridge Dictionaries Online (2011) Available online at **www.cambridge.org/** (accessed 13 May 2011).

Cashmore, EE (1988) *Dictionary of Race and Ethnic Relations*, 2nd edition. London: Routledge.

Clancy, A, Hough, M, Aust, R and Kershaw, C (2001) *Crime, Policing and Justice: The Experience of Ethnic Minorities. Findings from the British Crime Survey (Home Office Research Study no. 223)*. London: HMSO.

Collander-Brown, D (2005) Being with another as a professional practitioner: uncovering the nature of working with individuals. *Youth and Policy*, 86: 33–47.

Collins (1998) *Collin's English Dictionary*, 4th edition. Glasgow: Harper Collins.

Connell, R (1995) *Masculinities*. California: University of California Press.

Cooley, CH and Schubert, HJ (1998) *On Self and Social Organisation*. Chicago: University of Chicago Press.

Cottle, S (2000) *Ethnic Minorities and the Media: Changing Cultural Boundaries*. Buckingham: Open University Press.

Crosby, M (2005) Working with people as an informal educator, in Harrison, R and Wise, C (2005) (eds.) *Working with Young People*. London: Open University Press and Sage Publications.

Davies, B (2006) The place of doubt in youth work – a personal journey, *Youth and Policy, Special Issue: Muslim Youth Work*, No. 92, 69–80 Summer 2006. Leicester: National Youth Agency.

Denzin, NK (1989) *Interpretive Biography*. London: Sage.

Department for Education and Skills (DfES) (2003) *Common Core of Skills and Knowledge for the Children's Workforce*. London: HMSO.

Erikson, EH (1974) *Identity: Youth and Crisis*. London: Faber and Faber.

Fryer, P (1984) *Staying Power*. The History of Black People in Britain. London: Pluto.

Gandhi, M (1921) *Quotes of Gandhi* (compiled by Shallu Bhalla). New Delhi: UBS Publishers.

Giddens, A (1991) *Modernity and Self-Identity: Self and Society in the Late Modern Age*. California: Stanford University Press.

Giddens, A (1997) *Sociology*, 3rd edition. Cambridge: Polity Press.

González-López, JM (2002) A portrait of Western families: new models of intimate relationships and the timing of life events, in Carling, A, Duncan, S and Edwards, R (eds.) *Analysing Families: Morality and Rationality in Policy and Practice*. London: Routledge.

Gramsci, A (1971) *Selection from the Prison Notebooks*. London: Lawrence and Wishart.

Hall, S (1978) *Policing the Crisis*. London: Constable.

Hall, S (1992) The question of cultural identity, in McGrew, T, Held, D and Hall, S (1992) *Modernity and Its Futures: Understanding Modern Societies*, Book vi. London: Polity Press in association with the Open University.

Hamid, S (2006) Models of Muslim youth work: between reform and empowerment. *Youth and Policy*, no.92, Summer 2006.

Hannerz, U (1999) Cosmopolitans and locals in world culture, in Featherstone, M (ed.) *Global Culture: Nationalism, Globalization and Modernity*. London: Sage.

Hartman, P and Husband, C (1974) *Racism and the Mass Media*. London: Dans-Poynter.

Head, J (1997) *Working with Adolescents: Constructing Identity*. London: Falmer Press.

Held, A and McGrew, A (2000) *The Global Transformations Reader: An Introduction to the Globalisation Debate*. London: Polity Press.

Huntington, S (1996) *The Clash of Civilizations and the Remaking of World Order*. New York: Touchstone/ Simon & Schuster.

Inglis, F (2000) *Clifford Geertz: Culture, Custom and Ethics*. Cambridge: Polity Press.

Ingram, G and Harris, J (2005) Defining good youth work, in Harrison, R and Wise, C (eds.) *Working with Young People*. London: Open University Press and Sage Publications.

Jeffs, T and Smith, MK (2005) *Informal Education: Conversation, Democracy and Learning*, 3rd edition. Nottingham: Educational Heretics Press.

Johnson, E (2003) *Cultural Diversity: Cultural Diversity Guide*. London: Granada Plc.

Jones, O (2011) Unpeople? We used to call them working class. *The Guardian* 20 March 2011, **www. guardian.co.uk/commentisfree/2011/mar/20/unpeople-working-class-media-labour** (accessed 20 May 2011). (c) Guardian News & Media Ltd 2011.

Joseph, J, Akpokavi, KB, Chauhan, V and Cummins, V (2002) *Towards Global Democracy: An Exploration of Black Perspectives in Global Youth Work*. London: Development Education Association.

Khan, MG (2006) *Introduction to the Special Edition on Muslim Youth Work. Youth and Policy*, no.92, Summer 2006. Leicester: NYA.

King, A (1999) Architecture, capital and the globalization of culture, in Featherstone, M (ed.) *Global Culture: Nationalism, Globalization and Modernity*. London: Sage.

King, R (1999) *Orientalism and Religion: Post Colonial Theory – India and the 'Mystic East'*. London: Routledge.

Knapp, K and Knapp-Potthoff, A (1987) Instead of an introduction: conceptual issues in analyzing inter-cultural communication, in Knapp, K, Enninger, W and Knapp-Potthoff, A (eds.) *Analysing Intercultural Communication*. Berlin: Mouton de Gruyter.

Kroeber, AL and Kluckhohn, C (1952) *Culture, A Critical Review of Concepts and Definitions* (Papers of the Peabody Museum of American Archaeology and Ethnology, Vol. 47, No 1). Cambridge: Peabody Museum.

Laird, J (1993) (ed) *Revisioning Social Work Education: A Social Constructionist Approach*. New York: Haworth Press.

Lawler, S (2002) Narrative in social research, in May, T (ed.) *Qualitative Research in Action*, London: Sage.

Lawrence, D (2009) *The Fight for Justice for My Son Inspired Change. But Police Racism Survives. The Guardian* 24 February 2009, www.guardian.co.uk/commentisfree/2009/feb/24/institutional-racism-met-police (accessed 26 January 2011). (c) Guardian News & Media Ltd 2009.

Lewis, P (2002) *Islamic Britain: Religion, Politics and Identity among British Muslims*, 2nd edition. London: I.B. Tauris.

Lifelong Learning UK (2010) *National Occupational Standards for Youth Work*. London: Lifelong Learning UK. **www.lluk.org**

Meighan, R and Harber, C (2007) *A Sociology of Educating*. New York: Continuum International Publishing Group.

Modood, T (1992) *Not Easy Being British: Colour, Culture and Citizenship*. London: Runnymede Trust.

Moore, C (1991) Time for a more liberal and racist immigration policy. *The Spectator*, 19 October 1991.

Mukhopadhyay, AR (2007) Radical Islam in Europe: misperceptions and misconceptions, in Abbas, T (ed.) *Islamic Political Radicalism: A European Perspective*. Edinburgh: Edinburgh University Press.

Myers, K and Grosvenor, I (2001) Policy, equality and inequality: from the past to the future, in Cole, M and Hill, D (eds.) *Schooling and Equality: Fact, Concept and Policy*. Oxon: RoutledgeFalmer.

Nadel, SF (1951) *The Foundations of Social Anthropology*. London: Cohen and West

Nagarajah, S (2005) Mistaken identity. *The Guardian* 5 September, 2005 (c) Guardian News & Media Ltd 2005 **www.guardian.co.uk/world/2005/sep/05/religion.july7**

National Youth Agency (2004) *Ethical Conduct in Youth Work: A Statement of Values and Principles*. Leicester: The National Youth Agency.

National Youth Agency (2005) Ethical conduct in youth work: statement of values and principles from the National Youth Agency, in Harrison, R and Wise, C (eds) *Working with Young People*. London: Open University Press and Sage Publications.

O'Hara, M (2011) Sharp increase in suicide rates in Northern Ireland, *The Guardian*, (c) Guardian News & Media Ltd 2011 **www.guardian.co.uk/society/2011/mar/16/suicide-rates-northern-ireland** (accessed 16 March 2011).

Owen, N (2001) 'The Watermelon' from *The Magic of Metaphor – 77, Stories for Teachers, Trainers and Thinkers*. Carmarthen: Crown House Publishing Limited. **www.crownhouse.co.uk**

Parekh, B (2000) *The Future of Multi-Ethnic Britain: The Parekh Report*. London: Profile Books.

Peck, SM (1990) *The Road Less Travelled: A new Psychology of Love, Traditional Values and Spiritual Growth*. New York: Arrow Books.

Pilger, J (2001) *Globalisation: The New Rulers of the World*. Available at **www.inminds.com/new-rulers-of-the-world.html** (accessed 6 Apirl 2011).

Popple, K (2000) *Analysing Community Work: Its Theory and Practice*. Maidenhead: Open University Press.

Powell, E (1968) *Rivers of Blood*, Available at **www.toqonline.com/archives/v1n1/TOQv1n1Powell.pdf**

Quality Assurance Agency for Higher Education, (2009) *The Subject Benchmark Statement: Youth and Community Work*. London: QAA. Available at **www.qaa.ac.uk** (accessed 5 May 2011).

Ratcliffe, P (2004) *Race, Ethnicity and Difference: Imagining the Inclusive Society*. Maidenhead: Open University Press.

Ritzer, G (2000) *The McDonaldization of Society*. London: Pine Forge Press.

Roberts, J (1994) *Tales and Transformations: Stories in Families and Family Therapy*. New York: W. W. Norton and Company.

Roberts, J (2006) Making a Place for Muslim Youth Work in British Youth Work. *Youth and Policy*, No 92, Summer 2006.

Rogers, C (1961) *On Becoming a Person: A Therapist's View of Psychotherapy*. London: Constable.

Rogers, C (1983) *Freedom to Learn for the 80s*. Columbus, OH: Charles Merrill.

Rogers, C and Stevens, B (1967) *Person to Person: the Problem of Being Human, a New Trend in Psychology*. Lafayette: Real Press People.

Runnymede Trust, The (1997) *The Runnymede Commission on British Muslims and Islamophobia*. London: The Runnymede Trust.

Saeed, A (1999) The media and new racisms. *Media Education Journal*, 27: 19–22.

Saeed, A (2007) Media, racism and Islamophobia: the representation of Islam and Muslims in the media. *Sociology Compass*, 1: 443–62.

Said, EW (1978) *Orientalism*. New York: Pantheon Books.

Sallah, M and Cooper, S (eds.) (2007) *Global Youth Work: Taking it Personally*. Leicester: National Youth Agency.

Sanghera, G & Thapar-Bjorkert, S (2007) Gendering political radicalism, in Abbas, T. (ed) *Islamic Political Radicalism – A European Perspective*. Edinburgh: Edinburgh University Press.

Shank, RC (1990) *Tell Me a Story: A New Look at Real and Artificial Memory*. New York: Charles Scribner's Sons.

Sheridan, LP (2006) Islamophobia pre- and post-September 11th 2001. *Journal of Interpersonal Violence*, 21. 317–36.

Short, C (1999) *Trade Unions: Partners for Development – A Speech by Clare Short, Secretary of State for International Development at the TUC Congress*, Brighton: DFID.

Slattery, M (2003) *Key Ideas in Sociology*. Cheltenham: Nelson Thornes Ltd.

Smith, AD (1990) Towards a global culture? in Featherstone, M (1990) *Global Culture: Nationalism, Globalisation and Modernity*. London: Sage.

Smith, MG (1965) *The Plural Society in the West Indies*. California: University of California Press.

Soni, S (2006) Encountering 'Izzat' in Asian communities – a reflection on youth work practice. *Youth and Policy*, No. 90, 5–19 Winter 2006, Leicester: NYA.

Styles, MB and Morrow, KV (1995) *Understanding How Youth and Elders Form Relationships: A Study of Four Linking Lifetimes Programs*. Philadelphia: Public/Private Venture.

The Runnymede Trust (1997) *Islamophobia: A Challenge for Us All*. London: The Runnymede Trust.

Tylor, EB (1971) *Primitive Culture*, Vol. 1, 1958 edition. New York: Harper.

van Dijk, TA (1991) *Racism and the Press*. London: Sage.

Wardhaugh, R (1985) *How Conversation Works*. Blackwell: Oxford.

References

Watts, J (2007) Going under. *The Guardian*, Wed 20 June 2007. Available at **www.guardian.co.uk/uk/2007/jun/20/ukcrime.humanrights** (accessed 21 May 2011).

Whittaker, B (2002) Islam and the British Press After 9/11. Available at **www.al-bab.com/media/articles/bw020620.htm** (accessed 21 May 2011).

Woodward, K (1997) 'Introduction', in Woodward, K (ed.) *Identity and Difference*. London: Sage in association with the Open University.

World Commission on Environment and Development (1987) *Brundtland Report*. New York: United Nations.

Yolen, J (1986) *Favorite Folktales From Around the World*. New York: Pantheon Books.

Young, I (1990) *Justice and the Politics of Difference*. New Jersey: Princeton University Press.

Index